JavaScript Jems:
The Amazing Parts

First Edition

Mike James

I/O Press
I Programmer Library

Mike James: JavaScript Jems
1st Edition
ISBN Paperback: 978-1871962420
First Printing, 2020
Revision 0

Published by IO Press   www.iopress.info
In association with I Programmer   www.i-programmer.info

The publisher recognizes and respects all marks used by companies and manufacturers as a means to distinguish their products. All brand names and product names mentioned in this book are trade marks or service marks of their respective companies and our omission of trade marks is not an attempt to infringe on the property of others.

In particular we acknowledge that JavaScript is a trademark of Oracle.

Preface

"The competent programmer is fully aware of the limited size of his own skull. He therefore approaches his task with full humility, and avoids clever tricks like the plague."

Edsger Dijkstra

There is a well-known book called *JavaScript the Good Parts*, if you haven't read it, do. Even though it is now over 10 years since Douglas Crockford wrote it, it is still well worth the time and effort. This book was almost titled "JavaScript the Excellent Parts", but eventually the jems idea won.

Jem isn't a word you will find in the dictionary. Instead you will be redirected to Gem, among the definitions of which we find "something prized for its beauty and value". In English "gem" is pronounced "jem" and as I have always enjoyed alliteration "jem" stuck and is meant to convey qualities that are admirable for one reason or another.

This book is a "meditation" on the features that make JavaScript special and different from the run-of-the-mill languages that we are all familiar with. JavaScript isn't the standard C++ or Java clone. It isn't strictly-typed, it isn't class-based and it just does things differently.

It is object-oriented, but the desire to make it like the other dominant object-oriented languages results in much ugliness. *"Don't program JavaScript as if it was Java"* might be a good way to express this, but you could also say "don't criticize JavaScript because it doesn't do things the way Java does" - and for Java you can substitute your own favorite language.

While reading this book, don't simply cling to what you have been told, try to evaluate what the dogma gives you and at what cost.

Given that JavaScript has good parts then you can guess it has some bad parts or at least mediocre parts. These too will be pointed out along the way, as will differences or similarities to other programming languages.

There are, of course, many versions of JavaScript – after all it is subject to the periodic upgrade cycle typical of all programming languages. However, this book is about JavaScript in general. Where different versions do things differently this is clearly indicated. The fact the JavaScript is also called ECMAScript is taken as a basic assumption and not often referred to – I use ES, ECMAScript and JavaScript interchangeably.

This is not a cookbook of JavaScript techniques, although you will find some interesting techniques described. The intent is to create a set of readings that will be rewarding for the JavaScript programmer at any level. If you are a beginner then you might have to go away and find out about a feature whose knowledge is assumed.

This is not a JavaScript primer, a course, or a dummy's guide, but I hope it will broaden your horizons and enable you to see JavaScript for what it is - a unique and interesting language separate from a sea of uniformity that is class-based, object-oriented programming.

Finally, this is not a complete exposition of any aspect of JavaScript and you might well think of things that could have been included. If you do then email me with your suggestions for inclusion in a future edition.

Feel free to disagree at any point, but try to be clear about why you disagree.

During the preparation of this book I have benefited from helpful input provided by Ian Elliot, a close colleague on the I Programmer team and author of several JavaScript books also published by IO Press. My thanks are also due to Kay Ewbank and Sue Gee for proof-reading both text and programs. As with any highly technical book there are still likely to be mistakes, hopefully few in number and small in importance, and if you spot any please let me know.

Mike James
May 2020

This book is a revised and much expanded version of the series of *JavaScript Jems* on the I Programmer website:

www.i-programmer.info

To keep informed about forthcoming titles visit the publisher's website:

www.iopress.info

This is also where you will also find contact information, errata and updates. You can also provide feedback to help improve future editions

Table of Contents

Jem 0

Why JavaScript Is A Jem

"Better a diamond with a flaw than a pebble without."
Confucius

JavaScript is a much under-rated language.

The reason is probably that it seems to be a scripting language, its name suggests it is, aimed at non-programmers. As a result many JavaScript programs are horrible to look at and use few of the more interesting language facilities. JavaScript can be written in a one instruction after another without functions or objects and it often is.

Beginners treat it as a natural progression from tinkering with HTML and often pick it up as they go along. As a result not only is the typical JavaScript program lacking style, it often doesn't work too well either.

Unfortunately other problems arise when the experts get hold of it. JavaScript so flexible that you can turn it into almost anything you want to – so you will find JavaScript cast as C, C++, Lisp, Java, Scheme, etc. It can be used in a procedural fashion, object-oriented, functional, declarative or any discipline you care to apply to it, admittedly with variable amounts of success.

To compound all of these problems the official specification is very poor and often gives little guidance on how the language should be used. All this leaves the poor programmer wanting to use JavaScript in elegant ways with no option but to wade through exemplar code, usually in the form of widget libraries or similar.

The truth of the situation is that JavaScript is the only commonly used language today that isn't a clone of C++ or Java. It does things in a different way and this is both refreshing and educational. Its approach to objects is different. Its approach to data typing is different. Its approach to numerics is different. Its approach to asynchronous code is well … you guessed it … different.

In short, JavaScript is a jem because it is rare, sophisticated and much misunderstood. It has its problems, no question about it, but in most cases even its problems are the result of trying to do something difficult in a logical way.

The fact of the matter is that JavaScript isn't a crude scripting language with nothing but simple data types and basic verbs. It is a language with a philosophy and a style of its own. It even has a heritage in that it is based on Self, a prototypical object-oriented language, and Scheme, a functional Lisp derivative. It is more like Lisp than any other language and Lisp is held in much reverence by programmers who know it. Yet casual programmers who don't really get to grips with JavaScript proper and programmers experienced in other languages tend to call it a crude scripting language with nothing to offer the world. But with parents like these JavaScript can hardly be called "just a scripting language". It would be unrealistic, however, not to recognize that the language had to cope with limited resources early in its development and responded to a demand for it to be dumbed down so that non-programmers might manage to make some use of it.

As a result JavaScript is flawed, but arguably it's still enough of a jem to admire.

Object-Oriented and Dynamic

So what is special about JavaScript?

This is a question that is really only answered by reading the rest of this book, but it is worth a summary.

The first thing to say is that it is object-oriented, but its objects are dynamic. That is, you can create an object and add methods and properties to it at runtime. Indeed, you can even remove methods and properties, making the JavaScript object completely plastic.

This in turn means that JavaScript has a very weak notion of type. As an object can morph from one "type" to another by gaining and losing properties as required, there is no real notion of a type hierarchy and no need for one. In addition, there is no need and no provision for the class/object distinction.

In traditional object-oriented languages, objects are created by first defining a class, i.e a blueprint for an object. Then you create an instance of the class, i.e. an object. This is not a bad way to work with static objects and it fits in well with strong static typing, which is an approach many programmers think is good.

JavaScript, on the other hand, simply allows you to create an object - without the need for a class to act as a template. Once you have the object you can modify it as required by adding properties and even removing properties.

Of course, there are many who judge this particular jem to be a dud. Most disciplines of object-oriented programming insist on strong typing where objects are defined by classes which cannot change dynamically. Classes can inherit from other classes and this leads to a type hierarchy.

In theory, type checking using this hierarchy can find many errors, but all the errors that it finds are fairly easy to find at compile time and the approach is still subject to runtime-type errors. The consensus is that this approach to objects is more robust, but it can be argued that it simply introduces another level of complexity without delivering any important advantages.

This is not a widely held point of view and many programmers will swear that strong typing has saved them on more than one occasion and doing without it would be difficult. The problem is that this is a comparison of finding an error with perhaps not-finding the error and in truth the error wasn't that hard to spot, with or without strong typing. You used the wrong object, property or method.

There is also the claim that strong typing makes big projects easier to handle. This is often true, but only when typing is used as an alternative to good documentation and programming standards.

Prototype-Based?

In principle, JavaScript is also a prototype-based language where new objects can be created from existing objects, but in practice this is probably one of its weakest areas. In a prototype language, prototypes play the role of inheritance - one object serves as the basis for another object, providing it with a default set of properties and methods.

JavaScript originally implemented prototypical inheritance in a complicated way that makes use of a "helper" object, a function which acts as an object factory. The object factory creates instances of an object which provides a sort of basis for a type system - anything a given object factory creates is regarded as an instance of the same type. The only problem with this is that the instance can have properties and methods added or deleted at runtime which means that being of a particular type doesn't provide much information about the object unless you add some self-imposed rules.

In truth prototypes aren't really about inheritance, they are more about implementation efficiency. A prototype provides a packet of methods, i.e. code, that can be shared without duplication between any number of objects.

Modern JavaScript has provided additional and better prototype management options, but these haven't really entered the mainstream consciousness of the JavaScript community and old ways die hard. In modern JavaScript prototypes are a jem, which you'll find referred to repeatedly in this book.

Inheritance?

The object factory, or constructor, provides the mechanism of prototype inheritance. Any object created by an object factory uses the object factory's prototype property in an attempt to find any method or properties it doesn't implement directly. By setting the object factory's prototype property to another object you can implement inheritance and by prototype chaining you can also implement an inheritance hierarchy. This might sound like standard object-oriented inheritance, but it has its dynamic aspects. You can add properties and methods to the prototype object at runtime and so what is inherited can change at runtime.

This is inheritance, but not as we know it.

The problem is that the whole idea of the object factory and its role in inheritance and type isn't well thought out and it isn't complete. What is more, it isn't well enough understood by the average, or even expert, JavaScript programmer to really be used in a way that doesn't just mimic a broken implementation of classical inheritance.

JavaScript's dynamic objects are almost certainly best used without the help of type and with minimal use of classical inheritance. The problems that it seems to have are mostly due to the way we attempt to use it.

The key idea, as already mentioned, is that prototypes are not really about inheritance, they are about efficient sharing of code between multiple objects.

Asynchronous Programming

Asynchronous programming is the big programming problem that we fail to tackle head on. Languages like Python that come without a standard user interface don't naturally encounter the async problem and mostly it doesn't make an appearance in the language until much later – it isn't a core issue.

However, for JavaScript async code is a core issue because, right from the first program you write, you have to confront the use of the UI, i.e. the web page. By default your program runs in the same thread as the UI and this means if you block the thread then the UI, the web page, freezes. This is obviously not a good idea and so JavaScript is inherently event-driven. However, in the early days it didn't have any special facilities for asynchronous programming and so the standard paradigm of the "callback" was used for asynchronous behavior that did not fit into the event model. Callbacks are a terrible idea in that they are difficult to manage, make error handling harder and distort the natural flow of control.

As a first step to making async code natural in JavaScript, the Promise object was introduced. This was a jem in its own right, but soon afterwards it was combined with the new async and await statements that transform asynchronous code into something that looks like synchronous code. The way that Promises and async/await fit together to produce something amazing is a jem worth study, see Jem14. When added to the ability to start additional threads using Web Workers then the problem of asynchronous code in JavaScript is almost a solved issue.

Modern JavaScript is async-equipped.

A Functional Language

The second big aspect of JavaScript that tends to be overlooked is that it is a functional language. In it functions are not just "first class" they are "first class objects" - they have methods and properties and can be passed into and returned by functions like any other data type. Essentially a function is an object that carries a special method that is executed by the invoke operator i.e. a pair of round brackets ().

You can argue that having functions as first class objects is actually against the functional programming idea because it allows yet another way for functions to record state information. However, it might also be said that having functions as objects provides additional opportunities above and beyond the restrictions of functional programming.

As well as first class functions JavaScript also supports closures, recursion and dynamic modification of code. Closures are something that most beginners don't understand and when they do understand they have no idea how to make use of them. Closures make asynchronous programming, i.e. event handling, much easier and cleaner. If you look at most event handling in JavaScript you will find that this isn't the way that it is done, however, - another example of how JavaScript is misunderstood by many of its users.

If closures are generally misunderstood or misused, then what can you say about recursion and code modification? Recursion is a problem for the average programmer in almost any language and JavaScript is no exception. You may be able to use it, but do you know how to use it?

JavaScript does, however, omit a lot of very basic functional programming features. In particular there are no immutable data structures, with the exception of the String, and it lacks tail recursion optimization.

What all this means is that while JavaScript may not be a good language for strict functional programming, it allows the adoption of a functionally-oriented approach that has many of the benefits of a functional approach without the difficulties.

Extensibility

The fact that you can add many of the standard features of functional programming using a library brings us to the final topic - extensibility. JavaScript is an example of a minimal, but highly extensible, language. You can create JavaScript functions that mimic the features of just about any language. This has resulted in lots of big and useful JavaScript libraries - jQuery, script.aculo.us, Prototype, React, Lodash and so on. The only problem with this is that there isn't one big official JavaScript framework that you can devote your attention to. Choice isn't always a good thing in programming languages.

Shortcomings?

At the end of the story I have to be fair and point out that JavaScript has a lot wrong with it. It could do with some additional features such as access modifiers, threading, and the better facilities to manipulate the prototype pointer and control evaluation context. However, all of these are small additions that could be made without fundamentally changing the language. What is a more serious lack is the sort of IDE support we take for granted for "serious" languages such as Java or C#. In many ways it is not JavaScript that needs changing but its implementation and toolchain.

There are also well-intentioned, but poorly chosen, ways of working. JavaScript tries its best to be type-neutral and to not bother the programmer with irrelevant representational changes. What does it matter if the basic data type is 1.0, 1 or "1", they are all representations of the number one. However, JavaScript's data coercion can seem illogical unless you understand the logic. In many ways it is a flawed jem which is the source of a lot of criticism of the language.

Just remember the next time you approach a JavaScript task - you are working with a dynamic, untyped, functional,   prototypical, object-oriented language and not "just a script".

Many of these ideas are picked up again and explained in detail in the following jems. It is important to not approach what follows with an idea that there is a right way to do the job and there is no scope for doing things differently. Many of the perceived problems with JavaScript are the result of noticing that it doesn't do what Java, C++ or some other language does and in attempting to make it conform the ugliness just proliferates.

JavaScript isn't like other mainstream languages, but this doesn't make it wrong.

Jem 1

JavaScript Is Classless

"Object-oriented design is the roman numerals of computing."
Rob Pike

Modern JavaScript has a class construct but the real jem is that you don't need it and never did. JavaScript's approach to objects is simple, direct and all you need. You can try to pretend that JavaScript has class, but in fact it doesn't. But first what is "class" all about?

What Is An Object?

Because of the dominance of languages such as Java, C++, C# and so on, many programmers believe that the object-oriented approach involves class, inheritance and type hierarchies. Indeed, this idea is so strongly held that many will claim that JavaScript isn't object-oriented at all – it just has some half-baked object features. This isn't the case and as programming languages evolve there are many approaches to objects, not just the "standard model". In the case of JavaScript many argue that the "standard model" isn't all that correct and there is room for alternative approaches.

So what exactly is a JavaScript object?

This is a complicated question because the idea of an object serves many different purposes. At its most simple an object is a data structure called a struct or a record. The first data structure that most of us encounter is the array, which is a set of data accessed via a numeric index. For example, myArray[5] is the item of data stored in the array corresponding to an index of 5. A record or struct is simply an array where the index can be any type of data, not just numeric. The index is usually called a key.

For example:

```
myStruct["mykey"]=42;
```

stores 42 associated with "mykey". To retrieve the value you simply provide the key:

```
alert(myStruct["mykey"]);
```

This is all perfectly good JavaScript and if you try it out you will see 42 displayed. This type of array that allows a general key value retrieval method is often called an associative array or a hash and JavaScript is more or less built on the idea. Associative arrays are very useful and there is no better way to implement a lookup table, but what have they got to do with objects?

The simple answer is that with a slight change in notation an associative array becomes an object. Object (or dot) notation allows you to write array (or bracket) notation:

```
myStruct["mykey"]=42;
```

as

```
myStruct.mykey=42;
```

This syntactic change makes no difference to how things are implemented, but it makes a world of difference to how we think about things. When you use the "dot" notation you think of mykey not as an index or key into an associative array, but as a property of myStruct which is now best interpreted as an object.

With one simple syntax change an associative array, a data structure, becomes an object complete with properties. JavaScript makes the connection between the two ideas explicit where other languages cover it up.

So why is this view of the associative array as an object so important?

There are many different reasons and no one reason is the most important. At a simple level an object serves to group together data that belongs together. For example, a person object might have properties name, age and telephone number. This is really useful, but notice that it is no more than the associative array, the record or the struct gives you. The object idea really only begins to take off when you realize, or make clear, that properties can also be functions. Properties that are functions are often called methods, but there is a distinction to be made between function properties and true methods. See Jem 3 for more discussion, but the simple explanation is that function properties can do anything to anything, while methods generally are restricted to working with the data stored in the object.

For whatever reason, objects and object-oriented programming has been the dominant programming method for the last 50 years or so despite alternatives being proposed. However, as already mentioned, the form of object-oriented programming that has come to dominate programming isn't exactly what JavaScript offers. In particular, most object-oriented languages are class-based and this is what we need to look at next.

The Class Idea

Most object-oriented languages start from the idea that any object you want to create is going to be required in quantity. The reason for this, as we have just explained, is that objects are basically data structures. The majority of data structures are used repeatedly and not just once or twice. For example, data structures like arrays are not "one off" you generally create lots of them. In the case of an array in many languages you simply state a variable references an array and give the size of the array:

```
let myArray=new Array(20);
```

which in JavaScript creates an array with 20 elements.

Now consider that we want to extend this idea of an Array as the simplest object. What we need to do is find some way of specifying what methods and other properties are included and we need to do this in a way that lets us create as many copies or instances of this object as we need. The most common way of doing this is to invent the class. A class isn't an object, although in some languages it can be, even though this is potentially confusing. A class is a specification for what data and what methods an object has. For example, in Java (no relation to JavaScript of course) you would write something like:

```
class myClass{
   int myProperty=42;
   void myMethod(){};
}
```

which is a class that defines an object with one property myProperty and one method myMethod. Notice that myClass is not an object. It doesn't exist in your program as an object. To create an instance of an object that myClass defines you have to instantiate it:

```
myClass myObject = new myClass();
```

This creates an object called myObject and this new object has the properties and methods defined in the class definition. Now you can write things like:

```
myObject.myProperty=43;
myObject.myMethod();
```

where the first instruction stores a value in the property and the second calls the method as a function.

19

Notice that now you have defined a class you can instantiate as many objects of the same type as you need. While this idea has been introduced as a way of creating objects, it is important to realize that it is also the mechanism used by other languages to deal with data structures that aren't objects. For example, the C language, which isn't explicitly object-oriented, allows you to define a struct data type that has fields of a particular type and you can use this to create as many instances of the struct as you care to create. It doesn't make use of the class keyword or terminology but the mechanism is the same.

Also notice that a side effect of this approach is that the class can be considered as the type of the objects it creates. Every object you create using the class has the same properties and methods. This is the reason that the Java instruction has `myClass` twice. The first use defines the variable `myObject` as being of type `myClass`:

```
myClass myObject;
```

and the second creates an instance of `myClass` and makes `myObject` reference it:

```
myObject = new myClass();
```

and writing it as two instructions or one is valid Java.

The fact that the class mechanism introduces the idea of type is made use of in languages such as Java and C++to enforce strong typing. The idea is that if you state that a variable has to reference an object that is an instance of a particular class then you can check that this is true in practice. This is the essence of type checking. This is the simplest case of type checking but as we shall see inheritance makes things more complex and the rules for what types can be used with what variables are slightly more sophisticated than this.

If you believe that a language that has strong typing is better than one that doesn't then that is all you really have - a belief. There is very little evidence that strong typing helps catch errors that cannot be found by other simpler methods and it is a source of errors in its own right.

To really understand this you have to ask yourself what a type error is telling you. At the highest and most obvious level it is clearly telling you that you have used the wrong type, but what does this actually mean? If the type is wrong it means you are using an object that doesn't necessarily have the properties and methods that you have assumed it has. The error might be real, and in the code you might use something that the object doesn't have, or it might be that the object has the properties and methods you need, but is defined via some other, unrelated, class.

This is a contentious issue, but JavaScript is not strongly-typed, as we will see in Jem 2.

Twice Naming

The fact that there is a class and instances of that class is often confusing to complete beginners. They generally don't have enough understanding of the broader picture to see why class is necessary at all. They simply want to create an object and use it. There is also the irritating problem of having to use the same name more than once. Consider the need to define an input form object for borrowing books. In a class-based language you first have to define a class - what should you call it? The obvious name is bookform, but now what do you call the instance? You really want to call it bookform as well, but you can't. You might say that this is a trivial problem, but it is worth keeping in mind the saying that:

> There are two hard problems in computer science: cache invalidation, naming things, and off-by-one errors.

Having to find good names for a class and then a single instance makes the naming problem harder by requiring additional names for very similar things. The naming problem is particularly acute when you only need one instance of a class. It starts to feel as if the class is just an unnecessary extra entity that we could well do without. If you think that this is a small and irrelevant problem, you need to keep in mind that most classes that an application programmer, especially a beginner, creates are used for just one, or perhaps two, instances and having a class to cope with is an unnecessary complication.

The usual solution to the twice naming problem is to use a naming convention such as using upper case letters for all classes and lower case letters for all instances. So we would call the book form class Bookform and the instance bookform. You can also use prefixes and other ways of indicating a class - Cbookform and bookform say.

JavaScript provides a direct way to construct an object without the need to create anything extra like a class. This has many advantages when you only need a single object, not least the ability to assign a single meaningful name. When there is a need to create multiple instances you do need to create an additional related object – an object factory or constructor and once again the naming problem arises. There is simply no way to avoid the need to name both something that creates an instance of an object and the instance of the object that it creates.

Shared Code, Separate Data

There is a more subtle side to the class mechanism in that it is about more than simply creating multiple instances of an object. It provides a way to share the same code between those multiple instances. When you define a class there is a clear distinction between properties that are values and properties that are functions or methods - one you can use, the other you can call. When you use a class to create an instance, the instance generally needs its own copy of all of the properties that represent data, but providing a copy of the code to each instance would be wasteful. The data changes between instances, but the code stays the same. That is, an instance needs its own data but can quite happily share the code with other instances.

Defining the methods within the class allow it to be the repository of the code that all of the instances use. Notice the only advantage of this is efficiency. If you are going to create one instance of a class shared code is of no help as there is no one to share it with. If you create two instances it is of some help, and it gets more vital as you create more and more instances. If you define a Point class say and are planning to create thousands of point instances then it is vital that each instance doesn't have its own copy of the code and the class mechanism makes this automatically so.

In a class-based system instances all have their own data fields but share the code as defined in the class. In a non-class-based system each object you create by default has its own code and its own data. The reason for this is that each object is a single instance and shares nothing with any other object. In this sense every object is a singleton and there are no relationships between objects - they just happen to have the same code.

In most cases this is fine and code sharing isn't relevant. However, if you want many instances of essentially the same object then it can become more important. The simplest way of allowing code sharing is to have a single object that has all of the code that an object requires and pass any function call on to this code repository object. In JavaScript this code repository object is called a "prototype" and hence JavaScript is said to be a prototypical language. It is, but this is often mistaken as a statement that the prototype is JavaScript's inheritance mechanism. It can be used to implement inheritance, but it is much better considered as a mechanism for code sharing when you need multiple instances of an object. More about this idea later in this Jem.

Object Creation Without Class

JavaScript doesn't use the class mechanism. In JavaScript there is no concept of class and everything is an object. There are only instances and, as we will discover later, each instance stands alone – it is a singleton. At first this seems to complicate matters, but the fact of the matter is that most objects that we use are naturally singletons. That is, we mostly create objects that exist only as a one or a small number of instances. When we create a name and address form we generally don't instantiate lots of copies, often just one is enough. This is another reasons why beginners find the class mechanism of other programming languages difficult to understand and appreciate. Why create a class to create a single instance of an object?

In this situation JavaScript gets straight to the point - you create the object you want to use without the help of a class or anything else. This is because JavaScript makes explicit the link between an object and an associative array.

You already know multiple ways to create objects but it is worth making them clear:

- Use an object literal, also referred to as an associative array literal, and define properties in one step. In many ways this is the fundamental way of creating an object:

  ```
  let myObject={
              myProperty1:42,
              myProperty2:"deep thought"
  };
  ```

- Use an object literal and then add properties by assignment. Associative arrays are dynamic and allow the addition and removal of elements:

  ```
  let myObject={};
  myObject.myProperty1 = 42;
  myObject.myProperty2 = "deep thought";
  ```

- Use `Object.create` and specify a properties object. This is the most sophisticated way of creating objects and moves the emphasis back to the idea of a constructor, i.e. a function that returns an object:

  ```
  let myObject=Object.create(null,
                  {
                   myProperty1:{value:42},
                   myProperty2:{value:"deep thought"}
                  }
              );
  ```

Of the three, the `Object.create` method is the newest and most powerful way of doing the job and there is an argument that it should be the standard way of creating objects once you get passed the beginner stage. The first parameter can be used to specify the prototype for the object, more on this later, and the second parameter is an object that defines the properties. The property object has properties that are the names of the properties you want to define and each has another object, the descriptor, which defines that property. Notice that we are still using an object literal, or associative array, to create the new object.

The descriptor has the following possible characteristics:

- `configurable` - default false

true if and only if the type of this property descriptor may be changed or deleted

- `enumerable` - default false

true if and only if this property shows up during enumeration of the properties

If the property is a value then it can also have:

- `value` - default undefined

the value associated with the property

- `writable` - defaults to false

true if and only if the value can be changed by assignment

If the property is to be accessed via a getter and setter:

- `get` - default undefined

A function which serves as a getter for the property

- `set` - default undefined

a function which serves as a setter for the property

Note that you cannot use `get` and `set` in combination with `value` and `writable`.

You can see that `Object.create` allows easy control of how a property behaves and unless you are creating a very simple object it is worth using. It also demands a discipline of defining exactly the characteristics of each property rather than relying on defaults. As important is the ability to easily specify the new object's prototype, more of this later.

Multiple Instances

JavaScript objects are by their very nature singletons, but what if you want many copies of an object? For a class-based language this is easy – you simply use the class to instantiate as many copies of the object as you need. Every object that is created in this way is not only identical, but is considered an example of the same type.

So how do you create multiple copies of an object in JavaScript? The answer is surprisingly simple. You write the code to create the object in a function and call the function whenever you need a new instance. You can call the function an object factory or a constructor, but it really is this simple. In a class-based system the same technique is used to create multiple instances, but it is less explicit. A class-based language generally allows you to specify a constructor, which is a method that specifies how the new instance should be initialized – the actual construction of the instance goes on behind the scenes. JavaScript makes all of this explicit and the function creates the instance and initializes it according to the code you write. This is surprisingly simple and direct and an excellent way to discover how object creation works.

JavaScript provides a number of different variations on creating multiple instances. It provides the new operator, which can be used to make it easier to implement an object factory or constructor, but you don't have to make use of it - you can simply write a function that returns the object you need:

◆ Use an object factory function to create and customize an object:

```
function myFactory(){
            newObj={};
            newObj.myProperty1=42;
            newObj.myProperty2 = "deep thought";
            newObj.myMethod=function Hello(){
                            alert(this.myProperty2);
                    }
            return newObj;
            }

let myObject1= myFactory();
let myObject2= myFactory();
```

A slightly easier way of creating a factory function is to use the features provided by the new operator to create a "constructor":

◆ Use a constructor to customize and return the object:

```
function myConstructor()
            this.myProperty1=42;
            this.myProperty2 = "deep thought";
            this.myMethod=function Hello(){
                        alert(this.myProperty2);
            }
let myObject1=new myConstructor();
let myObject2=new myConstructor();
```

The use of new automatically creates an empty object {} and sets this to reference it. It also automatically returns this as the constructed object, but if you include an explicit return it simply disposes of the object that this references. The biggest problem with the constructor approach is the way it confuses the use of this. While in the constructor, this is set to reference the object being constructed - the instance. Within function definitions this doesn't have a value, the function isn't being evaluated. When the function is evaluated this is set to reference whatever called the function, usually the constructed object - the instance. In this sense the use of this is consistent, but it is confusing that one use of this is building the instance, i.e. adding properties and the other is defining methods - see Jem 4.

A more modern way of creating multiple instances is to use the Create method of the built-in object. This isn't usually considered as an alternative to using a constructor, but it provides the most sophisticated way of controlling the exact characteristics of the object you are constructing.

◆ Use object.Create with a suitable set of property descriptors.

```
MyObjectDescriptor={
                myProperty1:{value:42},
                myProperty2:{value:"deep thought"},
                myMethod: {value: function Hello(){
                                alert(this.myProperty2);
                        }
                }
        };
let myObject1=Object.create(null,MyObjectDescriptor);
let myObject2=Object.create(null,MyObjectDescriptor);
```

You can see that in this case it is the object which holds the property descriptors that determines the object that is created, and in this sense you can think of MyObjectDescriptor as playing the role of the class, but notice that each instance gets its own set of properties, including methods, in code. If you want to share code that should be in the prototype.

26

The Class Declaration

You can also use the `class` declaration introduced in ES2015 and lauded with bringing JavaScript up-to-date with more modern languages – it did nothing of the sort as it is equivalent to using a constructor. You can declare a `class` using:

```
class Point {
    constructor(x, y) {
        this.myProperty1=42;
        this.myProperty2 = "deep thought";
        this.myMethod=function Hello(){
                alert(this.myProperty2);
            }
    }
}
```

This can be regarded as a shorthand for:

```
function Point()
        this.myProperty1=42;
        this.myProperty2 = "deep thought";
        this.myMethod=function Hello(){
                alert(this.myProperty2);
            }
}
```

You can see that a class statement is simply "syntactic sugar" - it doesn't change the way anything works. It also allows programmers familiar with other languages to feel that everything is normal and class-based – it isn't.

You can think of the class declaration as a way of automatically generating a constructor. The important differences are that the class statement is not hoisted, and so has to occur before the first use of the constructor, and you have to call the Point function using `new`. Also the body of the class statement is executed in strict mode. If you don't provide a constructor then a default function is created which returns the empty object {}.

As well as class declarations there are also class expressions:

```
var Point=class{
            constructor(x, y) { …
```

The only difference is that `class` expressions allow a class to be redefined whereas a `class` statement throws an exception if you try to redefine it. The introduction of the class declaration and expression isn't a bad thing but it can confuse the beginner and mean that they never find out how JavaScript really works.

JavaScript Code Sharing

The idea of shared code was introduced earlier as one of the advantages of the class method - the class is a repository for the code used by all of its instances. By default JavaScript doesn't share code for the simple reason that even if objects are identical they aren't related in any way. It doesn't matter how you create a new object, it has all of the properties you specify and these are specific to the object. That is, if you create 100 objects and they all use the same code to do something and this code is defined directly within the object then there are 100 copies of the same code. These are not 100 instances of an object defined by a class, they are 100 independent objects.

Of course, JavaScript has to have a way to share code between objects for reasons of efficiency - what if it was 1000 objects or 10,000 objects? The original solution to the problem was the prototype mechanism. This is JavaScript's replacement for the class mechanism and it solves just the problem of code sharing - it doesn't introduce any clear notion of type.

Every object has a prototype object and if you try to use a property that the object doesn't have, the JavaScript engine will look to see if the prototype object has that property - if it does it is used as if it belonged to the original object. Notice that as the prototype object has a prototype, the system actually searches for missing properties down the prototype chain until it reaches a null prototype object.

This is a very good way to implement code sharing and to a lesser extent some aspects of inheritance. The only problem is that the early versions of JavaScript made it difficult to manually set the prototype object - you had to use a constructor to do it. The rationale was that the constructor allowed a weak notion of type to be introduced to JavaScript - all objects produced by the same constructor could be considered to be of the same "type". Of course, this has a lot of problems, not least of which is that objects can be dynamically modified and so two objects of the same "type" could still have different properties and methods.

The idea was that the constructor, indeed every function object, has a prototype property which can be set to an object that is to act as the prototype for any object created by the constructor. Put simply, the constructor, when called with the new operator, sets the object that this references to have the appropriate prototype so that the created object's prototype could not be changed and was inaccessible.

Some argue that the prototype should be immutable, but in a dynamic language like JavaScript this seems overcautious. Modern JavaScript not only lets you set the prototype object directly, but also lets you modify what it is via methods of Object.

It has already been suggested that `Object.create` is the modern way to create objects. Its first parameter specifies the prototype object to be used for the object being created. For example, we can define an object using two associated objects - the property descriptor and the object prototype:

```
let MyObjectDescriptor = {
                         myProperty1: {value: 42},
                         myProperty2: {value: "deep thought"}
                    };

let MyObjectProto = {
                 myMethod: function() {
                         console.log(this.myProperty2);
                 }

         };

let myObject1 = Object.create(MyObjectProto, MyObjectDescriptor);
let myObject2 = Object.create(MyObjectProto, MyObjectDescriptor);
```

The property descriptor is used to create the properties of the object and each instance has its own set of properties. The Prototype object is generally used to define the methods of the new object. In this case each instance doesn't get a copy of the methods as any method calls are simply delegated to the prototype.

Of course, you can wrap the call to `Object.create` in a function which acts as an object factory and this makes things look simpler from the outside. For example:

```
const myObjectFactory = function () {
                 const myObjectDescriptor = {
                  myProperty1: {value: 42},
                  myProperty2: {value: "deep thought"}
                 };
                 if (myObjectFactory.myObjectProto === undefined) {
                   myObjectFactory.myObjectProto = {
                        myMethod: function Hello() {
                                 console.log(this.myProperty2);
                        }
                 };
                 }
                 return
                   Object.create(myObjectFactory.myObjectProto,
                                          myObjectDescriptor);
         };
```

You can see that this object factory isn't working in the same way as a constructor. It creates a property descriptor and a prototype and then uses these to create the object via `Object.create`. It could be made slightly more

efficient by only creating `myObjectDescriptor` once, as is the case for
`myObjectProto`. This is only created the first time the object factory is called
and then stored in the `myObjectProto` property. As explained in the next Jem,
functions are objects and can have properties.

Consider the following use of the object factory:

```
const myObject = myObjectFactory();
const myObject2 = myObjectFactory();
```

We now have two objects which have their own properties, but share the
same code. If we call the method on both objects:

```
myObject.myMethod();
myObject2.myMethod();
```

we get the same result, i.e. `deep thought` is printed twice.

If we now change the prototype stored in the object factory:

```
 myObjectFactory.myObjectProto.myMethod=
            function(){
                      console.log(this.myProperty1);
                   };
```

and call the method on each object again:

```
myObject.myMethod();
myObject2.myMethod();
```

then, unsurprisingly, we see `42` printed twice - the two objects do use the
same function as their prototype.

Notice that if we had created the prototype object each time the object factory
was called then the code would not be shared because each object would
have its own separate and independent prototype and hence code. If you
comment out the if statement in the previous example and create the
prototype anew each time then you will see the difference. After:

```
 myObjectFactory.myObjectProto.myMethod=
            function(){
                      console.log(this.myProperty1);
                   };
myObject.myMethod();
myObject2.myMethod();
```

you will see `deep thought` and `42` printed as only the second object has the
object stored in the object factory as its prototype. The first object has the
original object created on the first call as its prototype.

You have to be very careful that you use the same object as a prototype when
the intent is sharing code.

To summarize:

- A good and efficient way to create objects that you are going to create multiple instances of is to use a property descriptor for its properties and a prototype object for its methods.
- Even if you don't use Object.create to generate multiple instances, the same rules apply. If you want shared code for the instances created then define all methods as the object's prototype object.
- If the intent is to share code, make sure that the same object is actually used as the prototype for all of the instances. Using different instances of the object doesn't share code.

Non-Prototype Code Sharing

An alternative to using the prototype mechanism is to explicitly create Function objects for each method and then assign them to properties. For example, the previous object implemented in this way would be:

```
const myMethod = function Hello() {
                console.log(this.myProperty2);
            };
const myObjectFactory = function () {
                        const myObjectDescriptor = {
                            myProperty1: {value: 42},
                            myProperty2: {value: "deep thought"}
                        };
                        const myObject = Object.create({},
                                            myObjectDescriptor);
                        myObject.myMethod = myMethod;
                        return myObject;
                    };
```

You can see that `myMethod` is defined as a standalone Function object and simply assigned to a property of the object being created in the object factory. The object instances that the factory creates all have a reference to the same Function object and so the code is shared. If you try:

```
const myObject = myObjectFactory();
const myObject2 = myObjectFactory();
myObject.myMethod();
myObject2.myMethod();
```

what you will see printed is `deep thought`.

To show that it is the same function doing the job you can add a property to the original and show that both instances have the new property:

```
myMethod.myProperty="Marvin";
console.log(myObject.myMethod.myProperty);
console.log(myObject2.myMethod.myProperty);
```

As should be obvious, both methods now have new property and you see `Marvin` printed twice.

Notice that one difference between this direct approach and the prototype mechanism is that it is more difficult to change the function used by all of the instances. That is, if you change a function on the prototype to something different then all of the instances that use that prototype use the new version of the function. If you change `myMethod` to a new function then all of the instances are unaffected and carry on using the old version of the function. In fact, to change them to use a new version is difficult because you have to update all of the instance properties to use the new function.

If the intent is code sharing, it is also important that the same function is used for all of the instances. That is, creating a function, even an identical function for each instance, doesn't share code.

ES2015 Class Code Sharing

The `class` construct introduced in ES2015 also allows you to share code. Any property defined within the class, but outside of the constructor, is assigned to the prototype. For example:

```
class MyObject {
        constructor() {
          this.myProperty1 = 42;
          this.myProperty2 = "deep thought";
        }
        myMethod() {
          console.log(this.myProperty2);
        }
 }
```

In this case `myProperty1` and `myProperty2` are defined on the instance, but `myMethod` is defined on the prototype and hence shared code.

The `class` construct is exactly equivalent to:

```
function MyObject(){
        this.myProperty1 = 42;
        this.myProperty2 = "deep thought";
 }
MyObject.prototype.myMethod = function(){
        console.log(this.myProperty2);
        }
```

and hence nothing more than syntactic sugar. The real question is - is it harmful syntactic sugar? Does it lead beginners to fail to understand the prototype mechanism and hence make bigger mistakes that are harder for them to find?

JavaScript doesn't have class and most programmers won't miss it once they realize how little they use it. Most objects are unique and if you do need a few instances then use an object factory or a constructor. JavaScript objects are classless and all the better for it. Object literals are jems.

Jem 2

The Inheritance Tax

"What is the object-oriented way of getting rich? — Inheritance."

Anonymous

Another aspect of the class mechanism is inheritance. You can use a class as the basis of another class. The new class has all of the properties and methods of the original class, it inherits from the original class, you can extend the new class by adding new methods and properties, and you can redefine inherited methods if they don't do the job. Before inheritance the common way to reuse code was to use copy-and-paste to duplicate code. Inheritance is dynamic in that if you change the original class the change is propagated to all of the classes that inherit from it. This used to be thought of as the best part of inheritance, but today things aren't so clear cut.

As JavaScript isn't strongly-typed, and it doesn't really do inheritance, some of the examples in this chapter are taken from Java. This is the only way to demonstrate what JavaScript lacks, or should I say avoids, by not supporting inheritance and typing. You can regard this as a Jem of omission. It is worth saying again that this is a contentious issue. Programmers familiar with other languages consider the idea that class, type and inheritance can be dispensed with as ridiculous. So much so that syntax that makes it looks as if JavaScript does support inheritance has been added to ES2015 and there are language "wrappers" like TypeScript that support typing.

Class As Type

In most class-based languages, classes are considered to be types and not objects. The fundamental purpose of the class mechanism is to create a "cookie cutter" template that can be used to stamp out as many instances of the class as required. However, as every instance produced by the class is the same, it leads on to the idea that class defines type.

In a class-based language declaring a class also creates a new data type. That is, in Java:

```
Class MyClassA(){
   lots of properties
}
```

not only creates a new class, it also adds the new data type, `MyClassA`, to the type system.

In this way of doing things objects are of a particular type, and variables have to be declared as a particular type, and a variable can only reference objects of that type. Now when you declare a variable of the type:

```
MyClassA myVariable;
```

the system knows what `myVariable` is referring to. This allows the system to check that when you write:

```
myVariable.myProperty
```

that `myProperty` is indeed a property defined on the type. If it isn't then you get a compile time error, which you can correct before it throws a runtime error.

Contrast this with JavaScript, or any untyped language, where `myVariable` can reference any object and hence you cannot deduce that:

```
myVariable.myProperty
```

is valid simply by reading it. You can usually deduce its validity by reading the rest of the program, however. Strong typing makes this aspect of static analysis easier, but this comes at a cost. Given that type occurs in two ways – a variable has a declared type and an object is of a particular type - at its simplest strong typing simply enforces the rule that a variable can only reference an object of its declared type. That is, an instance of a class has a type and only a variable of the same type can reference it.

JavaScript has neither of these two complications - variables are untyped and can reference anything and objects are just objects and there is no type information associated with them. This is a great simplification and should be considered a jem.

Hierarchical Typing

Things are a little more complicated in most class-based languages in that they implement hierarchical type. In this case inheritance can be used to create a type hierarchy.

For example:

```
Class MyClassB:inherits MyClassA{
 lots of properties
}
```

Now MyClassB has all of the properties of MyClassA plus whatever is added as part of its definition. MyClassB is said to be a subclass of MyClassA and, as it has all of the properties of MyClassA, you can use it anywhere you could use an instance of MyClassA. After all, typing is all about making sure that an object has the properties that you are using, and an instance of MyClassB has all of the properties of MyClassA and so it can be treated as such. MyClassB is also a subtype of MyClassA in the sense that it is also a MyClassA as well as being a new type all of its own.

So it is perfectly OK in most strongly-typed, class-based languages to write things like:

```
MyClassA myObject=new MyClassB();
```

and then proceed to use any properties that belong to MyClassA. This means that a variable can reference an object of its declared type or any subtype. If you make a mistake and try to use a property that MyClassA doesn't have, then the compiler will tell you about the error at compile time and you are saved a runtime error.

Virtual Inheritance

There is a complication of this simple picture of inheritance. Suppose MyClassB overrides, that is redefines, a method to be more suitable for what it is doing. Now when you write:

```
MyClassA myObject=new MyClassB();
myObject.myMethod();
```

which method is used - the one originally defined by MyClassA or the overridden version defined by MyClassB? In other words, is it the type of the variable which determines which method is called, or the type of the instance?

There is no correct answer to this, but most languages will call the method determined by the instance not the variable. This is usually called virtual inheritance following C++ and in this case it would be the method defined

37

in `MyClassB` that would be called. Interestingly C++ doesn't implement virtual inheritance by default and it would use the method defined in `ClassA` unless otherwise instructed.

Of course, in JavaScript variables don't have type and so the method called always depends on the instance.

Why Is Hierarchical Typing Useful?

Hierarchical typing is useful because it allows you to write partially generic methods. Simple strong typing only lets a variable reference a particular class of instances and hence any function you write will only process that one single class of object. This is far too restrictive as usually you want your function to work with objects that are similar, but not necessarily identical. For example, suppose you have a class hierarchy Animal and two subclasses Cat and Dog. As long as you only want to use the methods and properties of Animal you can use hierarchical typing to write a method that can accept Animal as its parameter and use it with objects of type Animal, Cat or Dog.

When you write a function that works with a type, it should also work with all of its subtypes. This is a consequence of the Liskov substitution principle which states that a subtype can always replace a type. However, this isn't always true. It is only true if we as programmers make it true. For example, it only works if we either don't override methods in subclasses or if we are careful to make sure that the overriding doesn't invalidate the substitution principle. It could be that we have created a new method in the subclass that simply doesn't work properly with the original class. Overriding methods potentially breaks the idea that you can use a subtype in place of the type and no amount of type checking is going to warn you of this.

Most languages have a single topmost supertype that all other types derive from – usually called Object or something similar. You can use this to write completely generic methods because a variable of type Object can reference anything. However, because of strong typing the only methods that can be used are those that Object has, which are usually very few and very basic. Using the Object type you can write completely generic functions that work with any object. Of course, as JavaScript doesn't have typed variables, none of this is necessary and any function that works with an object will work with all objects as long as they have the properties that are used in the function.

Inheritance As The Model

Why do we use inheritance at all, and why is it related to the idea of subtype? This is a complicated question and one that leads to arguments. The original idea of using objects was to model the real world. In the real world things are objects with properties, and even methods, that allow the object to do something. Introducing objects into programming was to make it more like an exercise in simulation. Indeed the first object-oriented language was Simula, a language for simulation. The idea is that in the real world objects are related to one another. The problem is that they are related in complex ways.

As we have already stated, in programming the most basic intent of inheritance is to allow code reuse. Code reuse doesn't have much to say about any type relationships. It is tempting to take the next step and to say that if objectB inherits from objectA then it is an objectA as well as being an objectB. A square is a square, but it is also a rectangle.

The Liskov substitution principle is the best known embodiment of this idea. It says that anywhere you can use an instance of a class, you can use an instance of any subclass. The reasoning is that the subclass has all of the methods of the base class and more. This is often true, but it isn't always true. For example, by our previous reasoning, a square is a subclass of a rectangle, but you can't use a square everywhere you can use a rectangle. The reason is that you cannot set the sides of a square to different values. There is a restriction on modifying a rectangle to make a square.

Restrictions and specializations spoil the neat idea that subtypes can be used in place of their supertype. What this means is that the Liskov substitution principle is more a theoretical simplification than a reflection of the world. This also makes strong typing an arbitrary theoretical decision when it come to rules for how class instances can be used. You can find ways to make subclasses always work as subtypes. For example, if you implement a square as a rectangle that still has two sides specified, you can retain all of the quadrilateral methods and enforce the equality some other way. This is far from natural.

There is also the problem that, in the real world, objects are related to multiple other objects. A square is a special case of a quadrilateral and it is an n-sided equilateral shape. You could try to model this by using multiple inheritance, but this is usually much more difficult than it seems when you first start to try it. This is the reason most other languages restrict themselves to single inheritance. Other languages add the idea of interfaces – essentially class declarations with no implementation. This allows for a limited form of multiple inheritance, but does nothing for code reuse, forcing programmers to return to copy-and-paste code reuse.

The problem is that the real world is often not modeled well by a single inheritance hierarchy, whether used with or without strong typing. This is the main reason that you will hear advice such as "prefer composition over inheritance". The idea that one object contains another object is in many ways an easier concept to work with. So, for example, a car object might contain a steering wheel object and four road wheel objects, which in turn contain wheel objects. However, this doesn't always fit, how does a square contain a rectangle object? Add to this the fact that current languages provide poor support for composition and it isn't so attractive.

It is claimed that the hierarchy of classes and object types is good because it mimics the way the world is organized. Things in the real world are supposed to be structured in the same way, i.e. hierarchical, and our code should follow this lead and be hierarchical. Of course, this isn't the case - the relationships between things in the real world are much more complicated than a simple hierarchy. In many cases hierarchical typing means that you have to force your model of the world into an inappropriate form. There are examples where the hierarchy fits. Many code libraries are built starting off from a primitive example of the type which is then refined in different ways, leading to a hierarchy that represents the range of objects that are available. However, most programmers don't create libraries and spend more time working with objects that have messy complex relationships and perhaps no relationships at all.

Inheritance or Composition

It is often difficult to work out the best relationships between objects. For example, is a circle a subclass of ellipse or vice versa? At first it seems obvious that an ellipse is a subclass of circle because a circle has one radius and an ellipse has two, so an ellipse is an extended circle class. However, you can think of a circle as a special case of an ellipse when the two radii are equal. If you choose to implement the circle as the base class (using Java) then the result is something like:

```
public class Circle {
    int radius;
    void draw() {
        draw a circle using radius
    }
}

public class Ellipse extends Circle{
    int radius2;
    void draw() {
        draw an ellipse using radius and radius2
    }
}
```

As drawing an ellipse is more complicated than drawing a circle, we need to override the circle's `draw` function so as to draw an ellipse. So really all we get from the `Circle` class via inheritance is a single property, `radius`, which is not a rich inheritance.

What is more, with virtual inheritance, the norm in most languages, the Liskov substitution principle is broken. If you were to write:

```
Circle myShape=new Ellipse();
myShape.radius=10;
myShape.draw();
```

then, despite `myShape` being a `Circle`, it is the `draw` method of `Ellipse` that is used which uses `radius` and `radius2` to draw the ellipse. Of course, `radius2` hasn't been set, and cannot be set because `myShape` is a `Circle` and doesn't have a `radius2` property. We could write the ellipse draw method to conform to the Liskov substitution principle, but this is another complication. In general, overriding any method potentially breaks the Liskov substitution principle and invalidates hierarchical typing.

Now consider implementing things the other way around. Starting from an implementation of `Ellipse` let's derive an implementation of `Circle` in JavaScript that doesn't even hint at inheritance and uses `class` so you can compare the two. First the `Ellipse`:

```
class Ellipse {
   constructor() {
     this.radius1 = 1;
     this.radius2 = 1;
   }
   draw() {
     draw an ellipse using radius1 and radius 2
   }
 }
```

As a circle is a special case, a restriction, of an `Ellipse` we can implement `Circle` very easily:

```
class Circle {
   constructor() {
     this.ellipse = new Ellipse();
   }
   draw() {
     this.ellipse.draw();
   }
   set radius(value){
     this.ellipse.radius1=value;
     this.ellipse.radius2=value;
   }
   get radius(){
     return this.radius1;
   }
}
```

Notice that in place of inheritance we have composition - now the `Circle` object contains an `Ellipse` object. Also notice that we need `get` and `set` to enforce the restriction to a circle.

There are lots of cases where composition is much more natural than inheritance which is why the advice "*prefer composition over inheritance*" has started to gain ground.

The theory of inheritance and hierarchical typing is satisfying, but not a good fit with the real world and thus is one of the areas of object-oriented programming that has come under attack. All of this is an argument that is slightly beyond the scope of this discussion, but the key point is that inheritance and hierarchical typing have not been proved to be better than the alternatives.

Inheritance and Extends

As repeatedly stated, JavaScript doesn't have class-based inheritance and doesn't have a hierarchical type system, despite attempts to add both. You can regard a prototype object as being a "base object" that the "derived object" inherits from, and sometimes this is a realistic thing to do. At other times, the prototype is just a way of sharing code between multiple objects. In fact, most of the time code sharing is the motivation for using the prototype.

To make the prototype look more like class based inheritance ES2015 introduced the `extends` keyword:

```
class B extends A{
 constructor() {
    super();
     ...
 }
```

which makes it look as if inheritance is in play. Again, however, this is syntactic sugar, but of a slightly higher order than we have encountered so far. The reason is that we want class `B` to have all of the properties and methods of class `A` before we start adding to it or modifying it. The problem is that class `A` has its own properties and methods, as well as those of its prototype object.

In JavaScript inheritance involves two objects not one.

The key to understanding what is going on is to realize that the `extends` keyword sets class `B`'s prototype to include `A`'s prototype in its prototype chain. So `extends A` is equivalent to:

```
B.prototype = Object.create(A.prototype);
```

This makes `B`'s prototype a null object which has `A`'s prototype as its prototype. This allows new methods to be added to the null object without modifying `A`'s prototype. After this step `B` also has all of the properties and methods provided to `A` by its prototype chain.

We now have to deal with A's own properties and to inherit these we have to use the `super` function call, which will call any method of the base object using `super.baseFunctionName()`. If you call it without specifying the function you are calling, the base class constructor is called and the result is set to `this`. That is `super()` is equivalent to:

```
this=new A();
```

This means that the new class B has all of the methods and properties of class A defined directly before you start adding to them. In this sense a class B object really does start out as a class A object. Notice that you can pass parameters to the base class constructor and, if you don't want the owned properties to be inherited, then you can avoid calling `super`.

At this point class B has all of the properties and methods, both its own and those provided by the prototype, of class A. This is how you can implement something like class-based inheritance in JavaScript with or without the `new class`, `extends` and `super` keywords of ES2015.

Is Class Harmful?

JavaScript, specifically ES2015, has class in name only as it is still an object-centric language. Does the attempt to import the idea of class into it matter? Is it just a syntactic ploy to simplify and make object creation seem more like what the majority of programmers are familiar with?

There is a sense in which this is true, but there are some negative effects. If you think in terms of class there is a tendency to see objects that have the same properties and methods as somehow being related or worse, "the same".

In JavaScript every object is a singleton and not an instance of some class. Each object has its own copy of the data and the code that operates on it, unless you go to a little effort to share the code. And more to the point, things that look like classes are in fact objects that are object factories. Covering up how things work is likely to lead to subtle and very difficult-to-find bugs.

A typical, though obvious, error caused by focusing on class is when two different objects that just happen to have the same properties and methods are are used as the prototype for another set of objects. Clearly only one of the two should be used as the prototype, but thinking of them as instances of a class makes them seem interchangeable. Similar mistakes are often more subtle than this.

In JavaScript there are only objects and every object is a singleton. This jem means that JavaScript is simple and direct in its approach to objects, but it also demands that you understand and use the facilities correctly.

Jem 3

Functions Are Objects

"Form follows function - that has been misunderstood. Form and function should be one, joined in a spiritual union."

Frank Lloyd Wright

This jem is just the fact that functions are objects. This is often repeated but little understood. In particular, when it is summarized as "functions are first class objects" it is too easy to miss the full implications and just conclude that you can pass functions as arguments to other functions. This is true, but there is so much more. A better title for this jem would be "Functions are just objects with some code", but this wouldn't be understood by all until they had read to the end.

JavaScript, inherently an unusual language, does its best to appear "normal". So when you first learn about functions you are told to use a "normal" way to define them:

```
function myFunction(a,b){
  var answer=a+b;
  return answer;
}
```

Yes, this looks like a function as you might define it in almost any language with perhaps slight variations in syntax. It looks as if you are defining a function that is just a block of code, but this isn't the whole story.

JavaScript functions are objects and this is clearly revealed by the alternative way of defining them, the function expression:

```
var myFunction=function(a,b){
  var answer=a+b;
  return answer;
}
```

This is often described as defining an anonymous function, but this is a bit misleading as in JavaScript all functions, and indeed all objects, are anonymous in this sense.

While the first version makes it look as if myFunction is the name permanently allocated to the function, no matter how you create the function you can treat myFunction as a variable and assign a new object to it. In this sense myFunction is not a fixed permanent name for the function.

Note: most JavaScript engines will take note of the name myFunction as assigned in the first version and report debug information about the function using the name – you can still assign to it, however, and break any association between the name and the function.

There is also a full constructor for a Function object;

```
var myFunction=new Function("a","b","var result=a+b;return result");
```

which defines the same Function object as the previous two expressions. There are some small differences but this isn't important in the present context.

It is important to always think of a function as just an object that happens to have some code that you can execute. That is, myFunction is a reference to an object just like any other and myFunction(*parameters*) executes the code associated with the object. Of course, the only objects that have code are function objects and so can be executed - they are callable objects.

OK, so a function, even if it sometimes doesn't look like it, is an object – so what?

There are three large consequences of this and the first is the best known:

1. You can use a function anywhere you can use an object. In particular you can pass a function to another function.
2. Function objects can be created within other objects and so have a lifetime independent of when they are executed and this is the reason for implementing closure.
3. Functions can have properties that exist even when the function is not being executed.

Let's look at each of these in turn.

Passing Functions

The first is the characteristic most often associated with "first class functions". As a function is an object you can use a function anywhere you can use an object. In particular, you can pass a function to another function. For example:

```
var myFunction=function(a,b){
  var answer=a+b;
  return answer;
}
var myAlerter(c){
  alert(c(2,3));
}
myAlerter(myFunction);
```

In `myAlerter`, `c` is a standard parameter and we pass `myFunction` as an argument. The variable `myFunction` is a reference to the function object we created and hence `c` is a reference to the same object. In the call to `alert`, `c(2,3)` calls the function passed into the `myAlerter` function.

Notice that there is another key idea here. If variable o references an object then o(*parameters*) calls the object as a function – which of course only works if the object is a `Function` object, aka a callable object.

As you can return an object from a function, you can also return a function object. For example:

```
var myAlerter(c){
   alert(c(2,3));
   return c;
}

var f=myAlerter(myFunction);
```

Following this `f` is a reference to the same function object as `myFunction`. It can be used simply by writing `f(1,2)`.

Lifetime And Closure

In most cases a function that returns a function usually creates the function it returns. For example:

```
var funFactory=function(myValue){
            var myAdd=function(a){
                    var result=a+myValue;
                    return result;
                }
            return myAdd;
        }
```

Notice that you can create functions within functions and so on. By the rules for local variables the inner function has access to the variables in the outer function, but not vice versa. That is, `myAdd` can use `myValue`, but `funFactory` cannot use `result`.

Now consider:

```
var myF=funFactory(3);
```

now `myF` references a function object with the code:

```
function(a){
   var result=a+myValue;
   return result;
}
```

If we call myF:

```
alert(myF(4));
```

the result is 7. This all seems perfectly reasonable until you start to look more closely at what is happening.

When we called funFactory it created a new function object. At the time that the function object was being created it had access to myValue because, as well as being a parameter, it is also a local variable. This is fine, but notice that when we call myF, which references the function object funFactory is not being executed – it finished when it returned the function object. By the usual rules, all local variables are destroyed when a function stops executing. So in principle, calling myF should result in an error as myValue no longer exists.

If this was the case we would have a problem in that now what a function does, or even if the function works, depends on when it is called. If it is called within funFactory then no problem because all the local variables it uses exist and are available to it. If it is called from anywhere else, after funFactory has finished running, then it crashes because the local variables that were available to it are no longer available.

A function should work irrespective of where is is called and so we are forced to invent the idea of closure. A closure captures the variables that are in scope when a function object is created. These captured variables exist for as long as the function object exists, i.e. they have the same lifetime.

As a side effect, variables in a closure are not accessible to any other part of the program. From the point of view of the rest of the program the closure variables were destroyed some time ago. This means that a function object can use variable that it has access to in a closure as a private variable.

Notice that closure is needed because functions are objects and they live for longer than just when they are being executed. In languages where functions are not objects there is no sense in which they exist when they are not executing and hence closure isn't a natural idea.

There is much more to say about closures and how they can be useful, but now you know why they are needed.

Function Properties

As a function is an object that just happens to be associated with some code that you can execute, a function can have properties. This is perhaps the strangest thing about function objects from the point of view of a programmer who is familiar with functions in other languages. In fact, it is so strange you very rarely see a function property actually being made use of in code.

For example:

```
var myAdd=function(a){
                  var result=a+myAdd.myValue;
                  return result;
                  }
```

You can see the general idea. The myValue variable is a property of the object myAdd which just happens to be a function. This looks wrong because the code of the function is using myAdd and myAdd.myValue before they are defined. If you think about it, this is not the case because the function only uses them when it is run, i.e. when it is invoked.

What matters is that myAdd and myValue are defined when the function is called:

```
myAdd.myValue=3;
alert(myAdd(4));
```

You can see that when myAdd is called, myAdd references the function object and myAdd.myValue is defined and now has a value. Again, this is another aspect of a function object living longer than its time executing.

It is also clear that myValue is playing the same role as in the previous example in providing the value the function adds to its parameter. In the previous case the value was provided from the outside world via a parameter that was included in a closure. In this case the value is provided as a property.

What is the difference? The key difference is that the property is public and available both while the function isn't running and when it is. The closure variable is only available to the function's code and hence only while it is running. This means you can change and access the property at any time, but the closure was set by the outside world just once, via the parameter.

You can use function properties for all sorts of of tasks, for example, error and status reporting:

```
var mySum=function(a){
                  var result=a*2;
                  mySum.error="something went wrong";
                  return result;
                  }
mySum(3);
alert(mySum.error);
```

Of course, in a real case you would have a conditional that set the property only when an error occurred. Also notice that you don't have to set up the error property before calling the function, but it is a good idea to do so. The dynamic nature of JavaScript's objects lets you add a property at any time. The downside is that if you try to use the error property before the function

49

has been executed you will get an error. Hence it is a good idea to initialize it when the function object is being created.

Function properties are not limited to simple values – they can be objects in their own right. In particular, they can be functions. This is another idea that causes difficulties if you are still thinking about functions as found in other languages.

What could function properties be useful for? Well, what about initialization:

```
var mySum=function(a){
                var result=a*2;
                mySum.error="something went wrong";
                return result;
            }
mySum.init=function(){
                mySum.error="";
            }
mySum.init();
mySum(3);
alert(mySum.error);
```

The only problem with this approach is that you have to remember to call the init function.

Another, and potentially more serious problem, is due to the fact that functions, indeed all objects in JavaScript, do not have fixed names. This is explained in detail in Jem 5.

If we assign something to mySum then the code in the function will fail because the new object isn't a function with a property called error. For example:

```
var mySumNew=mySum;
mySum={};
mySumNew(2);
```

fails because mySumNew might reference the same function object as mySum did initially, but within the code mySum now references an empty object and there is no mySum.error.

Using the alternative form of function declaration:

```
function mySum(){
                mySum.error="";
            }
```

is a sort of protection in that many JavaScript programmers think that now the name mySum is allocated to the function and this cannot be changed. It can and you get exactly the same problem, but as most JavaScript programmers believe that a function's name cannot change it is less likely they will try to.

The only real solution to this naming, or self-reference, problem is to create all function objects using a function factory:

```
var myFuncFactory = function () {
                    var self = function () {
                                    return self.myValue;
                              };
                    self.myValue=0;
                    self.error="";
                    return self;
                };
```

Notice that now you can create mySum using:

```
var mySum= myFunctionFactory();
```

and the code will work even if you change what mySum references because the code in the function doesn't make use of it. Instead it makes use of self, which, as it is part of the execution context of the function when it is created, it is part of the closure. This means that only the code in the function can access it and there is no chance of it being changed by accident.

This is why functions being objects that have some code associated with them is a jem.

Jem 4

Objects, Functions And this

"Nothing that surrounds us is object, all is subject."
André Breton

The mysterious this is a jem you can only appreciate if you understand objects and methods. Without understanding comes only confusion and resentment. However, it really is a simpler and elegant way of doing things. Let's start at the beginning, which is what many programmers never get the opportunity to do.

Why Objects?

In the early days of programming, programs were organized around functions, also called subroutines or procedures. You created some data and then you wrote functions to process the data. For example, if you had a list of values and you wanted them sorted into order you wrote a sort function. The function would accept the list as its first parameter and sort it into order as specified by the second parameter - ascending or descending:

```
sort(myList, order);
```

If you wanted to sort a different list then you simply reused the sort function. This works well but there are lots of problems in keeping track of the correct sort function to use. For example, do you need a special sort function to sort numbers and a different one to sort words? There is a sense in which the exact nature of the sorting operation is determined by the list itself. This is where the idea of objects starts. We can regard the list as an object that has properties, its length say, and methods, things it "knows" how to do. In practical terms this usually means writing the sort operation as:

```
myList.sort(order);
```

This is a very minor syntactic change but it creates the whole philosophy we know as object-oriented Programming, OOP.

The key thing is that now we assume that `myList.sort` is the correct sorting function for the type of object `myList` is. We don't have to search for the correct sorting function as it is now a property of the object.

This is the distinction between a function and a method. A function accepts parameters of particular types and performs an action. A method is associated with the type of data that it performs an action on.

So, instead of having to find out what the appropriate sort functions are:

```
sortNumbers(myList1,order);
sortText(myList2.order);
```

we can simply write:

```
myList1.sort(order);
myList2.sort(order);
```

and expect the correct sort function to be called as a method.

This is the most fundamental example of what in OOP is called polymorphism - the function changes to suit the type it is working with. This in itself is a huge simplification that makes objects and methods worth having.

Introducing this

Now consider the method calls:

```
myList1.sort(order);
myList2.sort(order);
```

Each sort function has to discover what objects it is working with. The first needs to sort `myList1` and the second has to sort `myList2`. You can think of this as a transformation back to the basic use of functions:

```
sort(myList1,order);
sort(myList2,order);
```

You can see that we can tell the function what object to process by passing it as the first parameter and this is the theoretical relationship between functions and methods.

There is a long history of calling this default first parameter `this` and so the definition of the sort function would be something like:

```
function sort(this,order){
```

The function would then sort whatever `this` turned out to be into order. Using the word "this" as the name of the first parameter is perhaps a bad choice as it makes writing about how it all works more difficult, but can you think of a better name? Some languages use "that" or "self" which are arguably better.

Within the function you would use the `this` parameter to work with the data. In some languages, Python for example, you have to write the function with a first `this` parameter and then when it is used as a method you don't specify `this` as the system does it for you. This means when you call something as a function you have to write:

```
sort(myList,order);
```

but when it is called as a method you write:

```
myList.sort(order);
```

and this can confuse beginners, especially when they are first making the transition from functions to objects - how many parameters does this function actually have?

The JavaScript Way

In JavaScript regarding a function as a method doesn't change the number of parameters it has because the first `this` parameter is always supplied by default, i.e. irrespective of whether the function is a method or not. While this does make things simpler, it means you are no longer free to choose what the first parameter is called - it is forever `this` - and it is always supplied, even if it isn't wanted.

That is, in JavaScript you would write the sort program as:

```
function sort(order){
```

and you have no need to explicitly write a `this` parameter in the function definition. You can rely on the system to provide a value for `this` automatically for you to use within the function:

```
function sort(order){
  this[0]=...
```

assuming that `this` is an array.

Calling the method using:

```
myArray.sort(order);
```

can be thought of as exactly equivalent to:

```
this=myArray;
sort(order);
```

Don't try to assign a value to `this` as it is controlled by the system and immutable, but this assignment is exactly what the system does behind the scenes.

That is, when you write:

```
object.function(parameters);
```

it is transformed internally into:

```
this=object;
function(parameters);
```

Every function in JavaScript has the default `this` parameter passed to it by the system, irrespective of whether or not it is a method. When called as a function, `this` defaults to the global object - `window` in a browser and `global` in Node.js. When called as a method, `this` is set to the object that the function currently belongs to. The value of `this` is usually referred to as the call context.

Consider the following example:

```
function print(){
    alert(this.name);
}

let myObj1={name:"Obj1",print:print};
let myObj2={name:"Obj2",print:print};
var name="global";

print();
myObj1.print();
myObj2.print();
```

The function `print` simply tries to display `this.name` and what is displayed depends on what the system sets `this` to. In the first call to `print`, as a function, results in `this` being set to `window` and so the function displays `window.name`, which is the global variable set to "global". The second call to `print`, as a method, sets `this` to `myObj1` and we see `Obj1`. The final call is another method call but this time `this` is set to `myObj2` and we see `Obj2` displayed.

It is important to realize that the JavaScript engine always sets `this` to the call context.

call & apply

Direct assignment to `this` isn't allowed but you can effectively assign to `this` using the `call` method that every function inherits from `Function`. When you use `call` you pass all of the function's parameters but with `this` as an additional first parameter.

For example:

```
sort.call(myArray, order);
```

In this case `myArray` is passed as `this` and you really do have the equivalent of:

```
this=myArray
```

You can also use the inherited `apply` method, the only difference is that in this case you can pass the rest of the parameters as an array:

```
sort.apply(myArray, [order]);
```

There is an argument that `apply` isn't needed any more as we can do the same job with `call` and the spread operator, ..., which when applied to an iterable, e.g. an array, spreads each element out as if it was a parameter. So we can write:

```
sort.call(myArray,...someArray);
```

and `someArray` is automatically spread, or unpacked, to form the parameters of the call.

Early and Late Binding

It is surprising that the `this` mechanism can achieve so much of what we need for OOP. A big problem with it as it stands is that it always "late bound". What this means is that what object a method deals with is determined at runtime, i.e. the method is bound to the object late in the proceedings.

You might think that this is exactly what you need but it is the cause of many errors whenever you pass a method to another function. The best known example of this problem is using `setTimeout` to call a function after a delay. All you have to do is supply the function and the time delay:

```
setTimeout(myFunction,1000);
```

and `myFunction` is called after 1 second (1000 milliseconds). Notice that `myFunction` is a reference to a function object and not a function evocation, i.e. not `myFunction()`.

Now consider what happens when you write:

```
setTimeout(myList.sort,1000);
```

Most beginners, and even the occasional well-versed JavaScript programmers, think of this is as "call `myList.sort` after 1 second". If this were the case then `this` would be set to `myList` and `sort` would sort the intended target, but this is not the case. The reference to the function object `myList.sort` is passed to `setTimeout` and when it is called `this` is set to whatever the call context is.

The correct way to think about this `setTimeout` is:

```
let tempSort=myList.sort;
setTimeout(tempSort,1000);
```

and when one second is up the call is:

```
tempSort();
```

which indicates that when `tempSort` is called `this` is set to the global object, not `myList`.

A very general phenomenon whenever you make a new reference to a function object, is that it changes the value of `this` when you call it to the new call context. This is a consequence of late binding and the solution is to use early binding where it is appropriate.

To early bind a function you can simply use the `bind` method to set `this`. For example:

```
setTimeout(myList.sort.bind(myList),1000);
```

Now when the one second is up sort will be called with this set to `myList`. The `bind` method takes a function object and augments it by storing a value of `this`. It is this augmented function object which is returned by `bind`. When the augmented function is called it sets `this` to the specified value and then calls the original function. That is, `bind` is equivalent to:

```
augFunc=myFun.bind(myObject,args){
          return function(args){
                  myFunc.call(myObject,args);
              }
      };
```

This is so close to what happens in the "real" bind method you can use it as the basis for a polyfil if you are working with an old browser.

The new Operator

One of the commonly heard criticisms of `this` is that it is used in different ways in different parts of JavaScript. In particular its use within a constructor and with the `new` operator is confusing. It isn't, but you have to think about it in the right way.

A Function object that can be called without `new` is callable. A Function object that can be called with `new` is constructable.

A constructor is a function which creates an object. It creates the object's properties and methods and anything else which needs attention and then it returns the constructed object. The `new` operator makes it easy to create a constructor.

When you write:

```
let myObj=new MyObject();
```

what `new` does is to create an empty object and set `this` to reference it. That is, it is conceptually equivalent to:

```
this={};
let myObj= MyObject();
```

The call context for the function that follows the `new` operator is a new empty object. You can also think of it as:

```
let myObj= {}.MyObject();
```

Perhaps it would be easier to see the consistency of the this idea if we wrote the `new` operator as:

```
let myObj= new.MyObject();
```

and think about `new` as just creating a new empty object which is the call context for the function and what is assigned to `myObj`.

The only other thing the `new` operator changes is that the constructor automatically returns `this`.

So the constructor:

```
function MyObject(){
 this.property1=42
 this.method=function print(){alert(this.property1);};
}
```

is actually conceptually the same as:

```
function MyObject(){
 this={};
 this.property1=42
 this.method=function print(){alert(this.property1);};
 return this;
}
```

You can see that within the constructor this is the call context - the new empty object which the constructor customizes. Within the method definitions this isn't the call context at all because the methods are being defined not invoked. That is, within function print this doesn't have a value at all because the function isn't being executed. Think of the function definition as a string that defines the method rather than something being evaluated now.

So even the new operator works in terms of the execution context and constructors are executed in the context of the new empty object that is created.

It is worth pointing out, in case you haven't read Jem 1: JavaScript is Classless, the obvious fact that you don't need to use the constructor mechanism if you want to create an object. A general object factory can implement creating an object by doing the work itself. For example:

```
function MyObject(){
 let that={};
 that.property1=42
 that.method=function print(){alert(this.property1);};
 return that;
}
```

In this case the factory creates the empty object and customizes it using the temporary variable that. Notice that inside the method definition we still need to use this as it is still the call context for the method when it is called. If you write an object factory in this way rather than using the new operator you invoke it with:

```
let myObj= MyObject();
```

However, if you do use new it makes no difference. On the other hand, if you don't use new with a true constructor things go very wrong because this is set to a call context that you didn't expect.

You can use the new.target pseudo-property to find out if a function has been called with new. If it has, new.target is a reference to the function. If new isn't used then new.target is undefined.

So to detect a constructor has been correctly called you can use:

```
if(new.target===undefined) deal with error;
```

You can also use new.target to correct the situation:

```
function myConstructor(args){
  if(new.target===undefined) return new myConstructor(args);
  rest of constructor
}
```

If the function hasn't been called using new the function is started over again using new.

The conclusion is that this is always the call context and if you understand the way it works there is no confusion.

Every Object Is An Anonymous Singleton

"We are Anonymous. We are Legion."
The activist group, Anonymous

There are many things that are difficult to unlearn when you start using JavaScript, but perhaps the hardest is the belief that objects are associated with an immutable name and that objects are related to one another in strange and perhaps complex ways. As Jem 1 explains, JavaScript doesn't have class, no matter how hard you try to force the mechanism on it. To really master JavaScript you have to change your world view so that you regard every object as an anonymous singleton. What exactly does this mean? Let's start with the way objects are referenced.

References

Most programmers, in most languages, treat objects as if they have permanent names, but mostly they don't. The reason is that what we often think of as the object's name is just a reference to it. In the early days of programming a variable was something that held a value - a number, say. Today variables more commonly are used to store a reference to an object. The best way to think of this is as the object being stored in memory separate from the storage allocated to the variable and the variable "points at" or references the object.

That is, when you write:

```
let myObject = Object.create(
                {
                    myMethod: function Hello() {
                        alert(this.myProperty2);
                    },
                {
                    myProperty1: {value: 42},
                    myProperty2: {value: "deep thought"}
                }
            );
```

or create an object in some other way, what happens is that memory is allocated to store the methods and properties of the object created and memory is allocated to store the variable myObject. The variable doesn't store the object itself, only a reference to the object, which takes a lot less space.

Notice that the object doesn't have a name. You access it using the reference stored in myObject, a variable which does have a name.

In other languages a reference would be called a pointer and accessing the object that was pointed at is called dereferencing. In JavaScript, and many other languages, we just take this for granted. The use of references with objects also leads to a distinction between value and reference semantics – although this is unnecessary in a language like JavaScript.

Value semantics is what happens when variables behave as if they store a value, i.e. the "object" is stored "in" the variable. For example, value semantics are often associated with numeric values:

```
let myVar1=42;
let myVar2=myVar1;
myVar2=0;
```

In this case the value 42 is stored in myVar1 and then copied into myVar2. When myVar2 is zeroed the value in myVar1 is unchanged, i.e. still 42. In other words, the value assignment makes a copy of the object being stored in the new variable.

Now compare this to reference semantics:

```
let myVar1={myProperty:42};
let myVar2=myVar1;
myVar2.myProperty=0;
```

In this case myVar1 is set to reference the object created and the assignment copies the reference into myVar2. Notice that the content of myVar1 is copied in both cases, but when you zero myVar2.myProperty it is the same object as myVar1 references and so myVar1.myProperty is also zeroed.

The difference in behavior is not due to any change in the way assignment works, but due to what is being assigned. In the first case a value is stored in the variable and in the second a value which is a reference to the object is stored. This causes beginners lots of problems until they finally understand the idea of a reference to an object.

It is particularly confusing in parameter passing.

For example, continuing the previous example:

```
function myFunction(p1){
 p1=0;
}
myFunction(myVar1):
```

In this case myVar1 isn't changed as JavaScript parameters are always passed by value and assigning to p1 has no effect on myVar1. This is true irrespective of whether myVar1 contains a value or a reference. However:

```
function myFunction(p1){
 p1.myProperty=0;
}
myFunction(myVar1):
```

does change myProperty if myVar1 is an object that has that property. Notice that if myVar1 doesn't have the specified property the result is an error and this is the case even if myVar1 is a value such as 42.

In JavaScript all values are objects.

There Is Only Reference - Boxing

Simple though it is, the use of reference rather than value is still the source of confusion. As the actual assignment mechanism is the same in both cases – the contents of variables are always copied – it is what is copied that varies, a value or a reference. This being the case it should be possible to think of it as a single mechanism and it is.

The key is to keep in mind that everything is an object and now consider the assignment that we previously considered a value assignment:

```
let myVar1=42;
let myVar2=myVar1;
myVar2=0;
```

Now think of the first assignment as myVar references the Number object 42. The second assignment assigns the reference to myVar2 now both variables reference the same object i.e. 42. Finally when we set myVar2 to reference Number object 0 obviously this has no effect on number object 42 or what myVar1 references. If you think of numbers as instances of the Number object then there is no value assignment. OK, you might want to argue that this is a very thin reinterpretation, so what about something a little more complicated like:

```
let myVar1=42;
let myVar2=myVar1+1;
```

Again there is no problem with interpreting this as reference semantics as long as you interpret the arithmetic expression as an object expression. As explored in Jem 6. an object expression takes the values of any objects within it, and combines them to create a new numeric object. Now `myVar2` can be thought of as referencing the new `Number` object 43.

You can explore this idea a little more – primitives have corresponding objects and these objects have properties. For example:

```
let myVar1=new Number(42);
myVar1.myProperty="deep thought";
alert(myVar1.myProperty);
let myVar2=myVar1;
alert(myVar2.myProperty);
```

Although this may seem a little strange, it is reference semantics in action with something you would usually consider a value. In this case 42 really is a `Number` object and we have added a property. Now when we assign to `myVar2` a reference assignment occurs and `myVar2` references the same 42 object that `myVar1` does. As a result you see `deep thought` displayed each time. What happens if you use a `Number` object in an expression? The expression makes use of the `Number` object's value and creates a new value as the result. So for example:

```
let myVar2=myVar1+1;
alert(myVar2.myProperty);
```

In this case `myVar2` is assigned to a brand new 43 object and the resulting alert displays `undefined` as the new object doesn't have a `myProperty`. Of course, this isn't exactly what happens. The 43 stored in `myVar2` is actually a value and not an object. The reason is that this is the way things have to be done for efficiency. However, this doesn't stop us from thinking about it in the way described.

Some languages make use of an idea called "autoboxing" to allow the illusion that everything is an object to extend to primitive values. Autoboxing promotes any value to a real object if you do something that needs the value to be an object. For example:

```
let myVar1=42;
myVar1.myProperty="deep thought";
alert(myVar1.myProperty);
```

First `myVar1` is stored the primitive value 42. When we use the value as an object in the second line, autoboxing converts the 42 into a full `Number` object, and everything works. However, if you try this out you will discover that the alert displays `undefined`. The reason is that JavaScript's autoboxing isn't persistent. As soon as possible, the primitive value is unboxed and returned to a primitive value, again for reasons of efficiency. This is a shame because it spoils the illusion that everything is an object.

JavaScript would be a more elegant language with persistent autoboxing.

There are only two occasions when JavaScript autoboxes a value. The first, as we have seen, is when you make use of a value as if it was an object, but this is a temporary boxing. The second is when you set `this` to a value in `call` or `apply`. This is because both `apply` and `call` assume that you are calling a method and need an object for this. The boxing only applies for the duration of the function call.

The point is that if everything is an object then there are only references and reference semantics.

The fact that we have to deal with the confusion of value semantics is purely because we have to use values for reasons of efficiency. In an ideal world values would not exist as a concept.

Objects Are Anonymous

So far everything is standard and much as you will find in almost any object-oriented language. Objects are not stored in variables - references to objects are stored in variables.

This also has the implication that objects don't have an immutable name associated with them. They are essentially anonymous. For example:

```
let center=new Point(10,10);
```

is often thought of as creating a new object, an instance of `Point`, called `center`. Of course, this isn't the case. The variable `center` is only associated with the instance of the object until it is assigned to reference another object. Other variables with completely inappropriate names could also reference the instance:

```
let button=center;
```

This is the case in languages, such as Java, that are class-based and strongly-typed. Strong typing, however, does insist that both `button` and `center` are of type `Point` and this is thought to be an advantage, even though it doesn't stop you using inappropriate names for variables.

The key idea, and this is true in most object-oriented languages, is that objects do not have fixed names - just references. In a class-based language at least the class name is fixed and gives an object some form of identity, but the idea that we name objects is myth - we name variables that reference them.

Functions Are Anonymous

This section really has nothing to add because, as long as you accept that functions are just objects and objects are anonymous, then it is obvious that functions are also anonymous. The problem is that we really don't believe that functions are anonymous. For example if you write a function:

```
function sum(A,B){
  return A+B;
}
```

then the function's name is sum and this reflects what it does. However, sum is just a reference to the function object and you can create new references and change the original. For example:

```
let mul=sum;
let sum=myObject;
```

Now you can call the summation function using:

```
mul(1,2);
```

and if you try to call the summation function using the sum variable you will see an error message. The reason for the function statement is to make JavaScript functions seem more like functions in other languages. The function declaration:

```
function sum(A,B){
  return A+B;
}
```

is very similar to:

```
let sum=function(A,B){
        return A+B;
      }
```

where the assignment of a reference to a variable is made explicit. However, there are some differences. The most important is that the function statement is hoisted, as explained in Jem 13, whereas the = assignment isn't. In addition, most implementations of JavaScript keep the name associated with a function declaration so that debugging is easier, i.e. errors are reported along with the function's name. In this sense functions do have fixed names, but not as part of the runtime behavior.

Everything Is A Singleton

As JavaScript isn't class-based and as objects are always dynamic, you really have to think of every object as a singleton. Clearly objects have similarities, but you cannot rely on any pair of objects being identical as you can in a class-based language. JavaScript objects are mutable unless you go out of your way to make them immutable.

This is often the biggest shortcoming claimed for JavaScript and yet class-based languages have their problems. The key advantage of most class-based languages is that when an object is created from a class is it immutable in the sense that it can't have methods and properties added or removed. Thus, if you know an object is of a particular class, you can be sure of what methods and properties it has - but how do you know what an object's class is? That is, if you have a reference stored in myObject, how can you know the class of the object referenced and hence deduce that it is safe to call myMethod?

The usual answer is strong typing.

We have already encountered the idea of strong typing in connection with the type hierarchy and inheritance in Jem 2, but there the emphasis was on the type of the object. Here it is the type of the variable that is all important. As already explained, in strong typing every variable has to have a stated class or type that it can reference. To make things more flexible, a variable is allowed to reference not only its declared class, but any class that inherits from that class, i.e. any subclass. The reasoning is that the derived classes have all of the methods and properties of the original class and so it is safe to use those methods and properties. This is hierarchical typing and it has already been described in connection with inheritance. In this case the focus is on checking that instances have the properties they should have at compile time.

This is all very reasonable and very attractive, but notice that it only works if the instances that are being assigned to the strongly-typed variables are known at compile time. If they are known then you can discover what properties and methods they have, even in a dynamic language like JavaScript. Strong typing catches errors, but only very trivial errors that are easy enough to find without accepting the restrictions and complications it introduces.

The two biggest complications are generics and variance.

Generics

Strong typing means that you cannot write generic algorithms. A generic algorithm is one that applies to a wide range of object types. For example, you might implement a sort algorithm that can sort any objects, no matter what type, as long as you can supply a comparison function.

There are two general ways of creating a generic method in a strongly-typed language. The first is that you can use the root of the type hierarchy, usually Object, to create variables that can reference any object type. In most languages a variable of type Object can reference any other type in the type hierarchy - as they are all subtypes of Object. In this sense Object acts as a completely general "untyped" reference. Except, of course, as the declared type is Object, you can't access any methods or properties of most of the objects it references unless you use a cast. So it isn't quite as powerful as an untyped reference.

The alternative is that you can use the language's generic typing facilities, if it has any. This essentially allows you to specify type as additional parameters.

Consider:

```
T add <T>(T a,T b){return a+b};
```

where <T> is a parameter that specifies the type of the object being used. When you use the generic method you have to specify the value of the type parameter. For example:

```
int c=add<int>(1,2);
```

uses the generic method with T set to int. That is, the function declaration is:

```
int add(int a,int b){return a+b};
```

Of the two methods, generics is better because it typechecks the method in the form in which you are using it. However, it is more complicated and it also has its limitations and complications in most implementations. Of course, if you drop typing then every function you write can be generic. Things switch around in this case and the problem becomes not making functions work with a wide range of objects, but restricting the range that they work with.

In fact, all JavaScript functions and methods are generic.

Variance

Variance is an advanced idea, but one that comes about quite naturally if you work with strong typing. We can extend the idea of subtype by simply turning the definition around. If you can use type B in place of type A then you can consider B to be a subtype of A or A>B. For example, a real or floating-point type can be used in place of an integer as you can always write an integer with a zero decimal part, so int>float.

Using this idea we can ask if one data structure based on a type is a subtype of one based on another type. For example, is an array of floats a subtype of an array of ints or vice versa. This is where the question becomes subtle. Consider the action of a set on an array element. You can obviously set an integer into a floating point array, but you can't set a float into an integer array without potentially losing the decimal part. So for a set action you can substitute a float array for an int array and hence int[]>float[] and a float array is a subtype of an int array.

Now consider a get action on the same pair of arrays. In this case the get has to return an int from the integer array and so you cannot use a floating point array in its place because get could return a non-integer. However, you can use an integer array in place of a float as its values just happen to have a zero decimal part. So, from the point of view of get, we have float[]<int[].

To summarize:

int > float

and for set:

int[] > float[]

but for get:

int[] < float[]

We say that for set the array is covariant as the subtype relationship is the same, but for get the array is contravariant because the relationship is reversed.

What does this mean? It means that if you are storing values in an int array then strong typing should allow you to use a float array in its place and if you are retrieving values from a float array you can use an int array in its place. If your reaction that this is quite mad - because you nearly always save and store values to an array - you would be quite right and Java, for example, a strongly-typed language, makes its arrays invariant, i.e. neither covariant or contravariant. In this case you can't use an array of a different type at all, even if it would work for some reason.

The way that in this discussion we have been using arrays generalizes to more complex data structures and to functions. In general, values that act as inputs are covariant and those that act as outputs are contravariant. These ideas are particularly important for parameters and return values in functions.

Now compare this complex approach to JavaScript's. As variables aren't typed there is no sense in which variance even arises as a concept. You can replace a data structure with any other because data structures aren't typed. To be more clear, all objects are equivalent and all algorithms are generic. When you write a function and use that function it is up to you to work out what you expect the objects involved in the transaction to conform to, and it is up to you to make sure that they do.

With JavaScript you can avoid the straitjacket of strong typing and apply controls to your objects that suit the purpose and this is a jem.

Is Strong Typing Bad for You?

Strong typing is a big restriction on how you work with objects and its only payback is that you can specify in your code what methods and properties an object has. Notice, however, that this only works if the object's type is known at compile time, and if its type is known at compile time then a compiler could check on what methods and properties the object has without strong typing.

In many cases strong typing can be thought of as "active documentation" where you are forced to say what objects can be used in an operation - usually a function call. Programmers generally don't like writing documentation and having the language itself provide some seems like a good idea but it leads to documentation like:

```
int sum(int, int)
```

which is fine when it is obvious what sum is doing to the `int`, `int` to give `int` but this is often not the case.

The magic thinking of "type-safe" programming has become the central dogma of object-oriented programming and yet it's rarely put to the test. All too often you will hear "*but that's not type-safe*" or "*there has to be a type-safe way of doing that*" without any explanation of what this means exactly and without any cost benefit analysis. There are benefits, but there really are costs.

JavaScript's approach to objects is simple, direct and just as manageable, as long as you take the time to test, comment and document your code. Of course, many programmers don't and this is the one big claimed advantage of strong typing - it forces you use to a minimal level of description.

In most cases it is enough to think of every JavaScript object as a singleton that might have the same properties and methods as other objects. When you create a point object then you have an expectation that it is going to have an x and y property and so on. If you use an object factory or a constructor then these expectations are made clear. If you use a prototype object for the object's methods then the object's intent is even clearer.

So how do you work safely without type safety?

- You can just ignore the problem and try to write correct code in the first place and correct the code if you get a runtime error. Most of the time this is adequate as you can check what methods and properties an object has by reading the code or by using a static analysis tool.

- You can write tests for the existence of a property or method before you use it. If you use a test library then the testing can be achieved without slowing down the production code as the tests are removed. Notice that if the object being used cannot be determined before runtime then you need to leave the test in the production code.

JavaScript programmers have to come to terms with the idea that the objects that they work with are dynamic, singletons and anonymous. Yes, it does take a little more discipline to write good quality code, but not much. The payoff is that prototyping is much easier and faster and you are spared all of the difficulties of strong typing and single inheritance type hierarchies. While not widely recognized this simplicity is another jem.

Jem 6

Objects Have Value

"Objects are what matter. Only they carry the evidence that throughout the centuries something really happened among human beings."

Levi Strauss

Sometimes it is useful for an object to have a default value so that it can be used in an expression such as object+1 and object+"hello world". In JavaScript this is really easy and it is an important general principle – every object has a value. This is another jem of a general principle, but it has to be admitted that by not quite applying it rigorously enough JavaScript slightly spoils it. This is perhaps one of the most criticized aspects of the language, although once you understand what is going on it is easier to forgive.

Default Value

Sometimes it is good for an object to have a value, or even more than one value. For example, suppose you have an object that represents an item in an order. The object may have a number of additional properties and methods:

```
item.name="widget";
item.tax=0.1;
item.price=10;
```

However, if you consider the primary property of an item to be its price you might want to write expressions such as:

```
totalcost=item1+item2;
```

meaning:

```
totalcost=item1.price+item2.price;
```

Similarly you might consider the item's name to be its primary string property and you might want to write statements like:

```
alert(item);
```

meaning:

```
alert(item.name);
```

You might argue that this isn't a good example of using default values and that it would be better to use the full property names. However, everything in JavaScript is an object and without default values we couldn't write even the simplest expression. For example:

```
var a=1+2;
```

looks like a traditional "*add 1 to 2 and store the result in a*" statement, but as everything in JavaScript is an object, what it actually says is:

"add the default numeric value of the first object to the default numerical value of the second object and set the variable a to reference this new object with the default value 3."

In practice, interpreting the statement in this way makes little difference to the outcome, but it does help understanding some of the other features. Every object in JavaScript has a numeric and a string default value and these are used in expressions.

If you find it hard to treat a number like 2 as an object, then perhaps an easier example is the JavaScript Date object which returns the date as the number of milliseconds from the start date when used as if it was a number, and a formatted date string when used as a string.

So how do you define a default value? The answer is surprisingly simple. When an object is involved in an expression the valueOf method is called which returns a numeric or Boolean value. The numeric or Boolean value is further type converted, if necessary, to make the expression work. If the object is part of an expression where a string would be required then toString is called.

So far this is nothing new and it just gives rise to the usual type conversion rules that you should know about. However, you can define your own valueOf and toString methods and these can be used to deliver custom default values.

valueOf

All JavaScript objects will supply a value when asked for one. In many cases the value isn't of much use and hence it tends to be overlooked as a useful feature. For example:

```
var myObject={
 valueOf:function(){
   return 20;
 }
};
```

Following this you can write:

```
var result=myObject*10;
```

and `result` will be `200`.

If an object has a `valueOf` function defined then it can be used to supply a value whenever the object is used in an expression and a numeric value is required.

What do you think you get if you write the simpler:

```
var result=myObject;
```

The answer is not that `result` is set to the simple value 20. This is an object assignment and `result` is set to another reference to `myObject`. This can be confusing because if you now try something like:

```
var a=result*10;
```

you will still see `200` stored in `a` because `result` refers to the same object as `myObject` and so `valueOf` is called to return `20` in the expression. In other words, `result` behaves as if it was 20 in an expression, just as `myObject` does. However, if anything changes `myObject` so that it returns some other value, then `a` will not equal 200 after the expression.

The same is true for numeric objects. For example:

```
var result=20;
```

can be thought of as setting `result` to reference an object with default value `20`. Then, when you follow this up by:

```
var a=result*10;
```

`a` is set to reference a numeric object that has `200` as its default value. When working with numbers you tend not to think about it in this way, but is is just as valid. The point is everything in JavaScript is an object and assignment is always object reference assignment.

This view also explains what happens when you try to assign to the default value of an object.

For example, what does:

```
myObject=3;
```

do? You might think, or hope, that it assigns 3 to the default value. Of course, it doesn't, because all assignment is via object references. This sets `myObject` to reference the numeric object `3`. That is, `myObject` no longer references the object that has a default value function, but a completely new object that has the default value `3`.

You cannot assign to any object's default value.

At this point you might bethinking that an object's default value is immutable, and this is almost true. An object's default value is immutable unless its `valueOf` method is modified. For example:

```
myObject.valueOf=function(){return 42};
```

changes whatever default value `myObject` returned to be 42. Similarly changes to any variables of properties that `valueOf` might use can change the default.

The `valueOf` function also works if a Boolean value is required. For example, if you change the definition of `myObject` to:

```
var myObject={
  valueOf:function(){
    return true;
  }
};
```

then you can write things like:

```
!myObject
```

which evaluates to `false`.

At this point you might be wondering how you can work out what to return from `valueOf` when you can't know how it will be used in an expression. For example, what if you you use the `Boolean` valued `myObject` in an arithmetic expression? Of course, there is nothing to worry about because JavaScript's type juggling, see Jem 7, will sort it out for you and `true` will be converted to the value 1. In the same way, returning a default value of 1 will be treated as `true` within a Boolean expression. This is very flexible, but you should always return a value that is appropriate for the meaning of the object you are working with.

toString

You may not need a separate `boolean` `ValueOf` type function, but you do need a separate string value function. The reason is that what an object should return may be fundamentally different when a string value is required. For example, if a string value is required the object may need to format a numeric value so that it can be displayed. The good news is that it is easy to set a separate default string value using the `toString` function. For example, let's add a `toString` function to the `myObject` object:

```
var myObject={
 valueOf:function(){
   return 10;
 },
 toString:function(){
  return "ten";
 }
};
```

Now what do you think displays if you try:

```
alert(myObject);
```

The answer is the string `ten` because `alert` expects a string argument.

Now what do you think you get if you write:

```
var result= myObject+1;
```

The answer is `11` because the addition requires a numeric value.

It shouldn't come as a surprise to learn that you don't have to return a string from `toString`. JavaScript has no way of enforcing a return type, so in practice if you return some other type of value it will be converted to a string before being used.

One of the most useful things that you can do with `toString` is to define something more informative than the default `object:Object` message that you see when you use `alert` or the debugging console. For instance, you can define a `toString` function that provides helpful debug information, as in:

```
toString:function(){
 return "myObject Current State:"+10;
}
```

The `toString` function works in exactly the same way as `ValueOf` – assignment is by object reference and you cannot assign a new string value to an object.

A Simple Example

To implement the earlier example of an `item` object with properties `name`, `tax`, `price` as a singleton or object literal you would use:

```
var item = {
 name: "",
 tax: 0,
 price: 0,
```

and to make `price` the default numeric property and `name` the default string property you would define two methods:

```
valueOf: function(){
  return item.price;
 },
 toString: function(){
  return item.name;
 }
}
```

The complete object is:

```
var item = {
 name: "",
 tax: 0,
 price: 0,
 valueOf: function(){
  return item.price;
 },
 toString: function(){
  return item.name;
 }
}
```

Now if we set some values in the properties and try to use item in an expression, you will find that the valueOf and toString are called as defined earlier:

```
item.name = "widget";
item.tax = 0.1;
item.price = 10;
alert(0 + item);
alert(item);
```

The first alert has an arithmetic expression which expects item to be a numeric value so valueOf is called and the result is 0+10, i.e. 10. Notice that, as alert expects a string value as its parameter, JavaScript kindly converts numeric 10 into the string ten. In the second alert the item parameter is supposed to be a string and so toString is called which returns the name and so widget is displayed. Of course, you can use an object factory or a constructor to create multiple copies of the class as you require.

Functions

Now we come to a tricky area. As already discussed in Jem 3, in JavaScript functions are objects and they can have properties and methods. They can therefore have toString and valueOf methods. What this means is that a function can return three different values depending on how it is used.

Consider:

```
function myFunction() {
 return 1;
};
myFunction.valueOf = function() { return 2; };
myFunction.toString = function() { return "A"; };
```

After this what does:

```
alert(myFunction);
```

display?

Answer: A.

What does

```
alert(myFunction+0);
```

display?

Answer: 2.

Finally, what does:

```
alert(myFunction());
```

display?

Answer: 1.

All perfectly logical, yet this is the sort of "quiz" used by programmers wanting to prove how poor and confusing a language JavaScript is. It also raises the issue of why bother using a function if general objects can return a value? The reason is fairly obvious but deserves some thought.

Functions Versus Objects

You have a choice of associating a value with an object as in:

```
myObject+1;
```

or you can define a function that does the same thing:

```
myFunction()+1;
```

The difference is that the function has a natural way to accept arguments. For example, you can write:

```
myFunction(10)+1;
```

but without defining it to be a function, you can't write:

```
myObject(10)+1;
```

In other words, objects can simply represent a value or a state. That value or state can be manipulated by the methods that the object provides, but it cannot be modified while it is being used in an expression.

A function, on the other hand, represents a relationship between input data and the result. Notice also that, while a function is an object, not all objects are functions and in this sense a function is a "bigger" object.

When should you consider using a value associated with an object? Some might reply "*never*" as it isn't a common pattern and could be confusing. However, it is a fundamental pattern in JavaScript as all apparent values are the default values of some object. Even if you think it is an obscure pattern, if an object represents data or something with state then it is a good approach.

Consider the JavaScript 5 `Date` object:

```
var d=Date.now();
alert(d);
```

The `toString` function returns the number of milliseconds since the date epoch. A `Date` object is an ideal example of when to use an object as a value.

Now that you have seen how to create default values, you can think up your own uses for them. In some situations they can simplify the use of your objects by allowing them to be used in expressions.

Perhaps the real jem here is the entire idea of every object having a default value and assignment being based on object reference - more in the next jem.

Jem 7

Numbers And Other Values

"1,2,3,4,5,6,7"

from Einstein on the Beach

Philip Glass

JavaScript has no integers! Well this isn't quite true, but it is another Jem often offered up as a criticism of the imperfect language. In fact, JavaScript takes a very futuristic approach to data and to values in particular. It is a tough act to pull off and there are some rough edges, but overall it works and it really is a jem. In the latest version of JavaScript the concept of number has been extended in a way that is practical, but not as elegant as the original approach. Here we discover that you can have the best of both worlds.

Objects, Values and Expressions

In Jem 6 we discovered that objects have a value associated with them and in Jem 5 we discovered that in line with the "everything is an object" idea even values are objects - some of the time. For reasons of efficiency values are usually stored as values rather than objects and only converted to objects when they have to be - usually called boxing. An object's value is generally processed into something else by use of an expression. Expressions are mini-programs that are designed specifically to allow values to be combined to give new values.

For example, an arithmetic expression involves numbers and arithmetic operators:

```
let answer=3+4*2;
```

There are rules about how expressions should be interpreted. In particular, we use the rules of operator precedence. Multiplication has a higher priority than addition and so we do the multiplication of 4 times 2 first and then add 3.

Notice you don't actually need expressions because you could just use function calls:

```
let answer = sum(3,product(4,2));
```

We generally find expressions easier to write and understand - a consequence of years of tedious education in arithmetic classes.

If you follow the "everything is an object" philosophy then you will be perfectly happy with the idea that an expression combines the values of objects and creates a new object as the result with the correct value. This is a logical, but not practical, way of implementing expressions and as a result we need to recognize things within the language that are not objects - primitive values.

Primitive Values

JavaScript has an unusually large number of types of primitive values. In principle we only need two - number and text. In fact you can argue that only one primitive, number, is actually needed as text can be represented by numeric character codes. You could say that every primitive value is a number, but this would be taking logic too far for practicality. In all languages we have primitive types that provide more variety than just numbers. JavaScript has seven different types of value that are not objects.

There are five types that have equivalent objects and can hence can be boxed. These objects have the primitive value as their `valueOf` result. First we have the three primitives that have been in JavaScript from the beginning:

- Number - a numeric value that can be boxed by a Number object.
- Boolean - a value that can be true or false and boxed by the Boolean object, see Jem 8 for more.
- String - a set of UTF16 coded characters boxed by the String object.

Two more are recent additions to the language and not all browsers support them:

- BigInt - integers with an arbitrary precision and boxed by the BigInt object.
- Symbol - an arbitrary unique value boxed by the Symbol object.

The new BitInt primitive is useful if you need to work with integers bigger than $2^{53}-1$ which is the range that can be represented by Number, as explained later. A BigInt literal is written with a trailing n, for example:

```
let bigint=1234567890987654321n
```

You can also use the `BigInt` constructor to create a value. All you really need to know about `BigInt` is that it has as many digits as needed to represent the value or the result of an expression. You can't use the `Math` object's methods with `BigInt`, but you can use the standard arithmetic operators and the bitwise operators with the exception of `>>>` and division truncates any fractional part. You can use `BigInt` when you need to perform computations to an unlimited precision. Of course, the amount of storage and time to compute increases with the number of digits.

`Symbol` is a difficult value to explain, but things like it exist in other languages so why not JavaScript. It is closest to the idea of a unique identifier and is used to create properties that have a unique and opaque key. To understand how this works you first need to remember that an alternative way of working with a property is to use array notation. That is:

```
myObject.myProperty=42;
```

is the same as:

```
myObject["myProperty"]=42;
```

This is an example of a key value pair with `"myProperty"` being the key and 42 the value and you can either write `object.key` or `object["key"]` to access the value. The importance of the array method of accessing a property is that the key can be any expression that evaluates to a string. So you can use:

```
let key="myProperty";
myObject[key]=42;
```

This ability to use a dynamic key for a property is very powerful but consider the problem of adding a property to an existing object. How do you know that the key you are about to use isn't already in use? This is the problem that symbols where introduced to solve. A symbol is guaranteed to be a unique key. You can't know what that key is but you can use it. For example:

```
let key = Symbol();
myObject[key]=42;
alert(myObject[key]);
```

creates a symbol value which is stored in `key` and then used to create and access a property. Notice that you can't examine the key value although you can associate it with a label that can be useful in debugging. Even though the key is theoretically a string, you cannot convert it to an equivalent `String` object or literal.

You can use a symbol in an object literal as long as you use the array access notation.

That is:

```
myObject={ [key]:42};
```

and not:

```
myObject={ key:42};
```

Notice that array notation works even if `key` evaluates to a string expression and not just a symbol. You can be sure that if you use `Symbol` to create a property then that property doesn't already exist. This means you can also create hidden properties that other parts of your code cannot access if they don't have the symbol. This makes it a safe way to add properties to existing objects. In the spirit of keeping `Symbol` properties hidden, they don't appear in iterations or other general attempts to access all of the properties of an object.

If you need to share symbols between different parts of your program then there is a global symbol registry which will store an identifier and the symbol. To create a key in the registry you use:

```
Symbol.for("name");
```

If there there is already a symbol corresponding to `name` then the symbol is returned. If it doesn't exist then a symbol is created and returned. This allows symbols to be shared across different scripts but notice that now that "name" is not unique. For example:

```
let key1=Symbol.for("myProperty");
let key2=Symbol.for("myProperty");
```

first creates a symbol in the registry and stores it in `key1` and then retrieves the same symbol in `key2`. Notice that the instruction retrieving `key2` could be in a completely different script. The symbol is identified by `"myProperty"` which you need to ensure is unique.

In addition there are two primitives that don't have object wrappers:

- ◆ `Null` - a single value `null`.
- ◆ `Undefined` - a single value `undefined`.

`Null` and `Undefined` are confusing. When a variable hasn't been assigned a value it is set to `undefined` and `null` is a value that is used to indicate that a variable doesn't reference anything. The difference between the two is that `null` is never assigned automatically to a variable - it is available so that you can signal that a variable is intentionally not referencing anything.

If you encounter a variable that is `undefined` then you know that it has been declared but not assigned to. If you encounter a variable that is null then you know that the variable has been assigned `null` because the programmer wanted it to be null.

Notice that trying to use a variable that hasn't been declared or assigned to generates a runtime error. For example, if `myVariable` hasn't been declared:

```
if(myVariable===undefined){
        alert("undefined");
}
alert("finished");
```

results in a runtime error and you don't see either of the alerts as the program ends. If the variable is declared then its value is strictly equal to `undefined` and you see both alerts:

```
let myVariable;
if(myVariable===undefined){
        alert("undefined");
}
alert("finished");
```

There is one more complication. If you try:

```
if(myObject.myProperty===undefined){
        alert("undefined");
}
```

then if `myObject` hasn't been declared you get a runtime error as in the first example. If `myObject` has been declared then the access to `myProperty` creates the property and sets it to undefined so you see the alert display `undefined`.

What do you use `null` for? The main use of `null` is to free a reference to an object. JavaScript uses automatic garbage collection to remove an object as soon as there are no references to it. If you need to explicitly allow the garbage collector to destroy an object you can do so by setting all the references to it to `null`, for example:

```
let myObject1={};
myObject2=myObject1;
myObject1=null;
myObject2=null;
```

and, if there are no other references to the object, it will be garbage collected by the system.

Integers Versus Floats

Now we have to return to look at the simplest of primitive values - the `Number` object. If you have programmed in any other language you will know that there is usually a distinction between numbers that have no fractional part, the integers, and those that do, the floats. After a while this all seems very natural, but my guess is that when you first met the idea it was as strange to you as it is to any beginner today. Try telling a beginner that you need to treat a number like 1 and 1.0 as different in some way.

Back in the early days of computing it was important to distinguish the needs of different numeric ranges, such as fractional versus whole numbers, for issues of efficiency. This is because the way numbers are represented changes depends on what sort of numbers you want to work with. If you can restrict your attention to integer values in the range 0 to 256 then only a single byte is needed to store the value, but if you also want a fractional part, e.g. 100.25, then you need more bytes to store the number. At this point I could go into detail about the many different types of numeric representation, but this is not desirable in an age of powerful computers. If you are going to do things that require efficient storage then you might have to consider such issues. If you have to write programs that work with hardware or low-level APIs then again you might have to worry about numeric representation, but in most cases how the computer does arithmetic should not be a concern.

The programmer should be able to write values into a program without worrying about issues such as range or fractional parts. This was the idea that JavaScript originally implemented and to do this it made use of only a single numerical representation. In more recent versions of JavaScript typed arrays and high precision integer arithmetic have been introduced, but these are specialized facilities and they can be ignored until they are needed.

The idea was that numbers and indeed all fundamental data should be as easy to use as possible. What this means is that you can write:

```
let myVar=3;
```

or:

```
let myVar=3.0;
```

and expect them to mean the same thing. JavaScript's philosophy is that you shouldn't make an issue of something that most beginners wouldn't see as an issue and in this case three is three, no matter how you write it.

If you know about integers and floating point numbers you will be worried by this idea because you know that these data types have different properties. An integer is a number with no fractional part and when you do arithmetic with an integer the result can always be represented as another integer - except for division. In other languages 1/2 is generally taken to be zero because integer division rounds down or truncates to zero. In JavaScript 1/2 is 0.5 and an integer has become a float. Beginners usually find this to be natural because for them 1 and 1.0 are the same number.

What then if you actually want to treat a number as an integer?

Sometimes in programming the logic forces us to use an integer. Actually what it does is force us to use integer division. Arithmetic operations for integers are the same as for floats with the exception of division.

JavaScript, unlike many other languages, doesn't have an integer division operator, but it provides a number of different functions which can be used to control the way division is performed. Notice that it is the operation that is different, not the numeric representation.

The function that is closest to integer division is `Math.trunc()` which simply chops off the fractional part as if it never existed. That is:

```
Math.trunc(1/2);
```

is zero no matter how you write the numbers and in general:

```
Math.trunc(a/b);
```

is integer division of a by b. For example:

```
Math.trunc(7/2)===3
```

If you want the remainder then use the remainder operator %. For example:

```
a%b
```

is the remainder of dividing a by b. For example:

```
7%2 ===1
```

In general for integers, the remainder satisfies:

```
a= Math.trun(a/b) *b + a%b
```

For example:

```
7= Math.trun(7/2) *2 + 7%2
 = 3*2 + 1
 = 7
```

This relationship holds even when the values are negative or fractional and it is the definition of the remainder:

```
a%b = a - Math.trun(a/b) *b
```

For example:

```
-7 = Math.trun(-7/2) *2 + -7%2
   = -3*2 + -1
   = -7
```

or:

```
-7.8= Math.trun(-7.8/2) *2 + -7.8%2
    = -3*2 + -1.799999999999999
    ≈ -7.8
```

Notice that as soon as we make use of a fractional part, calculations are only approximate. Also notice that remainder is not the same as mod as defined in most other languages, see later.

There are two other functions that will remove the fractional part and these differ in how they regard negative numbers. The `Math.floor` function will return the next smallest integer and `Math.ceil` function will return the next largest integer. For example:

```
Math.trunc(42.5) === 42
Math.floor(42.5)===42
Math.ceil(42.5)===43
```

At this point you might think that floor is the same as `trunc`. Now consider:

```
Math.trunc(-42.5) === -42
Math.floor(-42.5)===-43
Math.ceil(-42.5)=== -42
```

The difference between `floor` and `ceil` is because -43 is smaller than -42.

Finally there is the `round` function which returns the closest integer unless the fractional part is exactly 0.5 in which case it rounds in the positive direction.

```
Math.round(42.5)===43
Math.round(-42.5)=== -42
```

What all this means is that even though there is no integer type you can still do integer arithmetic and in most cases in a similar way to other languages.

Returning to the remainder operator % it is worth pointing out that the mod or modulus operator defined in most other languages is given by:

```
a mod b = a - Math.floor(a/b) *b
```

This gives the same answer as `a%b` for positive values, but it is different for negative values. Notice that JavaScript doesn't have a mod operator and you have to use the definition given above.

The Exact Range Of Integers

Another concern often expressed about the unavailability of an integer type is the lack of an explicit range that can be represented exactly. For example, an integer in C can store -32,768 to 32,767 in two bytes. Some think that because JavaScript doesn't have integers it is somehow inferior to this.

A Number in JavaScript can store plus or minus 9007199254740991 without loss of accuracy, i.e it will be accurate to every digit. Once you go beyond this range you don't get an error message or any other strange behavior, but you do lose precision. That is, if you add one to 9007199254740991 you do not get 9007199254740992. You can find out if a number is in the accurate range using the `Number.MAX_SAFE_INTEGER` property. Notice that the bitwise operators convert to a 32-bit representation before being evaluated and so in this case the maximum safe range is 2147483647.

As you can see, there is very little to be gained in introducing integers into a high-level language like JavaScript. The simplicity in only having one type of number is far more important than any efficiency gains of introducing integer storage. As modern floating point hardware is as efficient as integer arithmetic, all that is saved is a small amount of storage. If efficiency, or other concerns, makes using an integer type worth the effort then you can always turn to JavaScript's typed array.

Strings Can Be Numbers 2

Explaining to a beginner that 42 and 42.0 are different types of number is a complication that can be avoided. So is there a difference between 42 and "42". In fact this particular difference is something that really mystifies a beginner and this suggests that it too isn't a natural or desirable feature of an advanced language.

If you know another language like Java, C++, or just about any modern language, you will probably be very happy about the difference between a number and a string that just happens to look like a number, but this isn't the same as justifying the distinction. A modern advanced language should relieve the programmer of the tedium of having to worry about converting a string that looks like a number into a number. You could say that this is another example of "duck typing" - if a string looks like a number then it is a number.

This is where JavaScript's notorious coercion rules enter the picture. Programmers from strongly-typed languages find the idea that primitive types should be used in such a free manner laughable. It isn't laughable, it is a requirement of a truly modern next generation language, which needs to move our concerns away from the internal representation used for data to the meaning that data has for a human. We have already met the idea that JavaScript doesn't make a distinction between numbers on the basis of their representation, i.e. floats and integers are one, why not take the extra step and unify strings that look like numbers and numbers?

JavaScript coercion is deeply connected with its approach to objects. Everything is an object and when a value is needed in an expression then in principle the object's `valueOf` method is called. However, things are slightly more complicated because JavaScript has primitive values as well as objects. Primitive values in expressions behave as if their `valueOf` returned their literal value. Only when the entity is a real object is `valueOf` called. What this means is that if you try to define a custom `valueOf` for a primitive value it will not be called, unless you explicitly create a wrapper object.

For example:

```
Number.prototype.toValue=function(){return 1;};
alert(2*(42));
```

displays 84, even though the toValue method of Number has been redefined.
However, if you force the primitive to be boxed:

```
Number.prototype.toValue=function(){return 1;};
alert(2*(42).toValue());
```

you will see the result 2 displayed. The point is that toValue isn't called for
unboxed primitives, which means you cannot customize.

If the entity in the expression is a general object, then its toValue or toString
method depends on what the current operator is, i.e. numeric or string. If
neither return a primitive value then a runtime error occurs. If one of them
returns a primitive value, of any type, then this is used in the expression after
conversion to the primitive type required. An internal function is called to do
the conversion - ToNumber or ToString respectively. JavaScript tries very hard
to find a value of the correct type to use in an expression and this can seem
complicated.

ToNumber converts primitives to a number according to:

Undefined	NaN
Null	+0
Boolean	true -> 1 false -> +0
String	to the value the string represents or NaN
Object	use toValue or toString and apply ToNumber again

Notice that when ToNumber is called on a string it will return a numeric value
if the string represents a numeric value - this is how strings become numbers.
This is reasonable, but notice that the format for what is a valid numerical
value in a string is different to a numeric literal. For example a null string and
white space converts to 0. You can lookup the details of the grammar used for
the conversion in the ECMA standard.

The ToString internal function converts primitives to a string according to:

Undefined	"undefined"
Null	"null"
Boolean	true -> "true" false -> "false"
Number	to a String that represents the number
Object	use toString or toValue and apply ToString again

All of this works to give reasonable behavior in most situations. For example,
if you evaluate 42*obj then as the multiplication operator always requires a
number it expects obj.valueOf to return a number.

If what is returned is a primitive value then it attempts to convert it to a number. If it is an object then it will call valueOf again. If you try:

```
let obj={valueOf:function(){return 2}};
alert(42*obj);
```

you will see 84 displayed. However, if you return an object:

```
let obj={valueOf:function(){return {}}};
alert(42*obj);
```

you will see NaN for Not a Number because the valueOf returns a null object not a primitive value. If you try:

```
let obj={valueOf:function(){return "2"}};
alert(42*obj);
```

you will see 84 as the string has become a number. How does this work? In this case valueOf returns a primitive, but it is of the wrong type and the system automatically calls the internal function ToNumber to get 2.

For a more complicated example consider:

```
let obj = { valueOf:  function () { return {}; },
            toString: function () { return "42"; }
          };
alert(+myVar.valueOf()+1); alert(2 * obj);
```

In this case you will see 84. The reason is that first valueOf is called, but this returns a non-primitive so toString is called, which does return a primitive, but of the wrong type. This is converted to a number by the internal ToNumber function.

It also works for String expressions:

```
let obj={valueOf:function(){return 42}};
alert("The number is: " + obj);
```

In this case obj returns the number 42 but a string is needed for the concatenation operator and so the internal ToString is called. If you write obj1+ob2 then the operation is concatenation if either obj1 or obj2 is a string and toString is called if the other operand needs converting.

Complicated inner workings, but what happens is usually what you expect and want – usually, but not always.

WAT?!

All of this is perfectly reasonable when viewed in this way, but some of the decisions about what constitutes a valid number are a little strange. To programmers used to strongly-typed languages and explicit casting they are seen as extreme defects. So much so that a notorious conference video called WAT?! amused an audience with a catalog of terrible code with unexpected results. For example:

```
+"".valueOf()
```

returns 0. That the null string should convert to zero fits in with the ideas of truthy and falsey, see Jem 8, but it can also seem illogical that something that isn't a valid number, i.e. a null string converts to a valid number - zero.

Most of the WAT?! examples, however, were concerned with built-in objects, which have perfectly reasonable `valueOf` and `toString` methods, but when used in extreme cases and in combination produce surprising results. One of the best known examples is:

```
[]+[]
```

This is easy to evaluate once you know that the `toString` method of `Array` returns a comma separated list of elements. For example:

```
[1,2,3].toString()
```

evaluates to "1,2,3".

Now that we know this we can evaluate the sum of two empty arrays. The `valueOf` method of the first empty array is called and this returns the entire array object, which isn't a primitive value so its `toString` method is called and this returns the null string - the list, a comma-separated list of its elements, is empty. As this first element in the expression is a string, the + is taken to be concatenation and so the `toString` method of the second empty array is called which returns another null string. Now the two null strings are concatenated and we have:

```
[]+[]=""
```

or put into words "the sum of two null arrays is a null string". Is this weird?

As another example, consider:

```
[] + {} = "[object Object]"
```

where "a null array plus a null object" gives [object Object]. Is this weird?

You should be able to work out why this is the case, but the null array becomes the null string, as in the first example. This means the + is concatenation and so the null object's toString method is called, which returns the string [object Object] which is the default if you don't define a custom toString. The null string and the [object Object] string are concatenated giving the result.

These are unexpected and not particularly useful "edge cases" of JavaScript's approach to unifying data types. The payoff is the simplicity in handling the vastly more common cases of non-null arrays and non-null objects and in being able to construct your own objects with values.

Is this a jem? Yes, I think it is, but a slightly flawed one.

Truthy And Falsey

"You can't handle the truth!"
A Few Good Men
Aaron Sorkin

JavaScript takes an interesting view of logic, the way that it is implemented and what you can achieve using it. Instead of just thinking about AND and OR as logic tables, you can think of them as variations on the procedural if..then..else. So, if you don't know about the active approach to logic read on, it is another jem.

Truth Tables

The traditional way of thinking about Boolean or logical operators is in terms of a truth table.

For example the truth table for the OR operation, i.e. || in JavaScript, is:

A	B	A||B
F	F	F
F	T	T
T	F	T
T	T	T

with T=true and F=false.

If you try this out using:

```
A=true;
B=false;
if(A||B) alert("The expression is TRUE");
```

you will see that the result is indeed true as the line starting T,F suggests.

Thinking about logical operations as truth tables makes them seem somehow static - and certainly not part of the flow of control of a program. However, this is just an illusion. Logic functions and branching of the flow of control are deeply related - so much so that they are the same thing.

The first difference between JavaScript and other languages is the fact that it uses a concept of "truthy" and "falsey". All values in JavaScript can be treated as if they were Boolean values. The values 0, null, undefined and the null string are falsey and they behave in logical expressions as if they were false. Everything else is truthy and behaves in logical expressions as if they were true. So, for example, you can write:

```
A=20;
B=null;
if(A||B) alert("The expression is TRUE");
```

and still see the TRUE message displayed because A is set to a truthy value and B is set to a falsey value which results in a truthy value.

Active Logic

Things are even stranger than just truthy and falsey values. There is another way to interpret Boolean logic that gets closer to the active or procedural notion of programming.

Take a look at the logical table for OR again:

A	B	A||B
F	F	F
F	T	T
T	F	T
T	T	T

You could interpret it as saying

"return the first value if it is true and return the second value otherwise".

In more usual programming terms:

```
if A then A else B
```

or as a JavaScript function:

```
function or(A,B){
  if(A) {
    return A;
  }else{
    return B;
  }
}
```

When you first see this form of the OR truth table it comes as something of a shock. We are so familiar with thinking of logical operators as just that - operators - that to see OR expressed in if..then..else form is almost disturbing. However, you can't object as it really does work - try it out and see.

This rule gives you exactly the same truth table when the values are Boolean, but consider what you get if the first value is numeric. For example using 0 for falsey and 20 for truthy as the first value, and the second as a string with "" and "Hello" being falsey and truthy respectively gives:

A	B	A||B
0	""	""
0	"Hello"	"Hello"
20	""	20
20	"Hello"	20

This looks very strange, but you can see that A||B returns B if A is falsey and A if A is truthy. Using the if statement equivalent of A||B makes what is happening clear and shows that:

```
result=A||B;
```

is the same as:

```
if(A){
  result=A
}else{
  result=B
};
```

For example:

```
A=2*6+9;
B=null;
alert(A || B);
```

displays 21 because the first variable is truthy, but:

```
A=null;
B="hello";
alert(A || B);
```

displays "hello" because A is falsey.

This example also gives us some idea of what this could be use for - default values. For example, consider the following function:

```
function test(a){
  a=a||"default value";
  alert(a);
}
```

If you don't remember, or don't want, to set the a parameter then it is undefined when the function starts to run and hence it is falsey and is set to default value. That is:

```
test();
```

results in default value being displayed. If you set the parameter then it is a truthy value and a remains unchanged.

Notice, however, that if you pass in a falsey value, such as the null string "" or 0, then these will also be replaced by default value, which might not be not what you intended.

The nullish coalescing operator ?? introduced in ES2020 is intended to improve on the way that the OR operator || behaves when setting a default. It is a logical operator that returns its right-hand operand as long as the left-hand isn't nullish, i.e. null or undefined. It behaves in a similar way to OR, but it doesn't work with the full range of falsey values. Its "truth" table is:

A	B	A??B
nullish	b	b
a	b	a

That is, if A is nullish the result is B, but if A is anything else the result is A. Typically you can use ?? to assign a default value more safely than with OR:

```
let myVariable=myValue ?? 42;
```

This sets myVariable to 42 if myValue is null or undefined, whereas:

```
let myVariable=myValue || 42;
```

sets it to 42 if myValue is falsey, i.e. 0, "", etc.

A better version of the test function for most purposes is:

```
function test(a){
  a=a??"default value";
  alert(a);
}
```

which would only set a to the default if it really was omitted and not just a falsey value.

Lazy Evaluation

There is yet another small and subtle point. Consider:

```
A || B
```

Notice that if the first value is truthy then its value is returned and the value of the second term is irrelevant. JavaScript takes advantage of this fact and saves time by not even bothering to evaluate the second term if it isn't needed. This is generally called lazy evaluation.

For example:

```
A=1;
A=A||test("function called");

function test(a){
 alert(a);
}
```

As A is truthy there is no need to evaluate the second term and hence the `function test` is never called. On the other hand if A is zero or any other falsey value, the function is called.

This sort of lazy evaluation can help you avoid runtime errors. The basic idea is that you write something as the first expression that evaluates to truthy when the second expression should not be evaluated. For example, JavaScript throws a runtime error if you try to access a method on a null object:

```
A=null;
A.method();
```

but we can easily check to see if a variable is null using:

```
!A||A.method();
```

in this expression !A. i.e. not A, is truthy if A is null and hence we never evaluate `A.method` if A is indeed null. You can avoid using the ! (NOT) operator (see later) by expressing the same idea using the && operator.

ES2020 introduced the optional chaining .? operator which detects attempts to call a method on an object that doesn't exist. If you write:

```
A.method.?();
```

then the optional chaining operator will test that `A.method` exists before attempting to call it. If it doesn't exist then the return value is `undefined`. The advantage over using AND or OR is that A has to be nullish, `null` or `undefined`, rather than falsey for the default to be returned and the method to be unevaluated. You can use multiple optional chaining operators in a fluent call, see Jem 12.

AND &&

All of the ideas that we have just encountered with respect to the logical OR operator apply to the AND operator. The usual truth table for AND, i.e. && in JavaScript, is:

A	B	A&&B
F	F	F
F	T	F
T	F	F
T	T	T

which we can now interpret as truthy and falsey values as for the OR operator.

You can reinterpret the table in an "active" way and formulate the AND operation as:

If the first expression is falsey then the result is the first expression.
If the first expression is truthy then the result is the second expression.

You could also interpret it as saying:

"return the first value if it is falsey and return the second value otherwise".

You should also be able to see that the AND operation:

```
result = A&&B;
```

is equivalent to the `if` statement:

```
if(A){
  result=B
}else{
  result=A
};
```

If you think about this for a moment, you should be able to see that (!A)&&B is "almost" the same as A||B in that both give the value B when A is false. However it isn't identical because when A is true (!A)&&B gives the logical opposite of A||B. That is, (!A)&&B is false but A||B is true if A is true.

The exact equivalence is given by one of De Morgan's laws of logic and it reveals that:

```
(!A)&&B  = !(A||!B)
```

You can use the AND operator in much the same way as the OR operator and it too uses lazy evaluation - that is, if A is false then B is not evaluated. This enables us to rewrite the protection against a runtime error given earlier as:

```
A=null;
A&&A.method();
```

thereby avoiding the use of a NOT.

NOT !

Finally we come to the NOT Operator, ! in JavaScript. This works in the same way as the other logical operators, but it only has a single operand and also works with truthy and falsey values:

A	!A
T	F
F	T

It is also worth knowing that NOT converts all truthy and falsey values into `false` and `true`, i.e. proper Boolean values. That is, `!null` is `true`, `!0` is `true` and so on. So while:

`"Hello" || 0`

is "Hello"

`!"Hello" && 0`

is `false`.

If you think about it, what other interpretation of !"Hello" could you use in this case.

You can think of converting truthy and falsey values into Boolean values as a second important use of NOT. Most of the time, however, its main use is to detect when a variable is falsey. For example:

```
A=null;
if(!A) alert("A is null or falsey");
```

will flag the fact that A doesn't exist i.e. null or undefined but it also detects if A is falsey. If you really want to detect that A is `null` or `undefined` then it is better to use the nullish coalescing operator ?? introduced in ES2020. see earlier. Using this the example can be written:

```
A ?? alert("A is null or undefined");
```

Now you will only see the alert if A is nullish and not if it is falsey.

Of course there is no lazy evaluation with a NOT as it has only one operand and that has to be evaluated to work out its truth value.

Ternary Expressions

You may have encountered the JavaScript ternary expression before, but regarded it as something special and not part of the whole logic of the language, but seen in the light of the way AND and OR are implemented it makes a lot more sense. The ternary expression is just another example of active logic. That is:

- `A || B` returns the second expression if A is false
- `A && B` returns the second expression if A is true
- `A ? B : C` returns B if A is true and C if A is false

In terms of a truth table this too is just a logical function but one with three inputs:

A	B	C	A?B:C
F	F	F	F
F	F	T	T
F	T	F	F
F	T	T	T
T	F	F	F
T	F	T	F
T	T	F	T
T	T	T	T

In this case it is the "active" interpretation of the logic that makes more sense than the "passive" truth table.

We have already noted that the `&&` and `||` operators are the equivalent of if statements. That is:

```
result=A&&B;
```

and:

```
result=A||B;
```

are the same as:

```
if(A){
  result=B
}else{
  result=A
}
```

and:

```
if(A){
  result=A
}else{
  result=B
}
```

It is interesting to notice that the ternary expression is also the equivalent of an if..else statement.

That is:

```
result=A?B:C
```

is the same as:

```
if(A){
  result=B
}else{
  result=C
};
```

This also means that the if and the if..else statements are just logical functions with the truth tables given earlier, although this is not the way we usually think about them.

Active logic and lazy evaluation make a great deal of sense out of some aspects of JavaScript that might otherwise look strange and arbitrary. JavaScript isn't the only language that has a ternary operator and understanding it in terms of active logic makes it seem much more natural.

The Comma

"I was working on the proof of one of my poems all the morning, and took out a comma. In the afternoon I put it back again."
Oscar Wilde

Such a small thing to be a jem but JavaScript's comma operator deserves a second look. Not every comma in JavaScript is an operator - in fact most of them aren't.

The Basic Comma ,

The comma operator , fits in with a set of expression operators and it can be useful, but it has a tendency to be used in ways that confuse rather than clarify. Part of the reason for this is that it is a comma , and commas have other meanings in JavaScript. To be 100% clear, the comma is only a comma operator when it acts on two expressions:

```
left-hand expression , right-hand expression
```

where *expression* is something that involves other operators, variables and functions, i.e. something that works out to a value.

What does the comma operator do? It evaluates each of the expressions, starting with the left-hand expression, and returns the value of the right-hand expression, for example:

```
a = (1, 2);
```

stores 2 in a. Of course, the 1 and 2 are standing in for any complicated expression you care to think up, and you can use string expressions, functions and so on.

But why the parentheses? The answer is that the comma operator has the lowest priority of all the JavaScript operators and without the parentheses the expression would be parsed as:

```
(a=1), 2;
```

which ends up storing 1 in a and throwing away the result of the right-hand expression.

If you use more than one comma then, by the rules of operator precedence and left associativity, the result is that each expression is evaluated in turn from left to right and the last one is returned as the result. That is:

```
(exp1, exp2, exp3, and so on expN)
```

evaluates exp1, exp2, etc. and returns expN as its result.

Side Effects

For simple comma expressions like:

```
a = (1, 2);
```

the value of the left-hand expression is always lost - so why bother? The answer is that some operators have side effects and most functions have side effects. Side effects are something that matters a lot in functional programming as we will discover in Jem 16, but meanwhile, put simply, a side effect is something that isn't just its result that is changed by a function when you run it. For example, you can use:

```
a=(console.log(1),console.log(2),console.log(3),4);
```

and you will see 1 2 3 printed on the console and 4 stored in a. The printing of values on the console is a side effect of calling the log function.

Of course, given function calls and assignments are also statements, we can use the semicolon:

```
console.log(1);console.log(2);console.log(3);a=4;
```

This is because semicolons separate statements and commas separate expressions, and in some cases statements are also expressions. There are places where you can only use commas, but often you have a choice. The problem this causes is that some programmers choose to use a comma just because it looks cool and this is just confusing.

This Is Not The Comma You Are Looking For

One reason for confusion is that there are lots of places where commas are just separators. For example, in object literals:

```
var obj={a:0,b:1,c:function(){}};
```

the commas are just separators and the same applies in arrays:

```
var arr=[1,2,3,4];
```

Again the commas are just separators.

Perhaps most confusing of all is the var declaration. For example in:

```
var a=1,b=2,c=3;
```

the commas are just separators, not comma operators. The reason is that this var statement is a declaration and is an initialization equivalent to:

```
var a;
var b;
var c;
a=1;
b=2;
c=3;
```

Things like a=1 is an expression; the value of the expression is, in this case 1. This allows you to write things like:

```
a=b=1;
```

which is equivalent to

```
a=(b=1)
```

However:

```
var a=1;
```

isn't an expression and doesn't have a value. Rather, it contains an expression because the initialization is of the form:

```
var variable=expression;
```

or:

```
var var1=exp1,var2=exp2 and so on...
```

This is subtle, but if you are following you can see that just by adding a pair of parentheses we can turn the previous var example into something that does use the comma operator:

```
var a=(1,b=2,c=3);
```

What do you think is stored in a, b and c?

The answer is that a holds 3, b has 2 and c has 3. The statement is of the form:

```
var a=expression;
```

and *expression* is:

```
(1,b=2,c=3)
```

which, by the rules of the comma operator, evaluates each sub-expression in turn, throws away each of the results except for the last, which is the value of the expression. Notice that the b=2 and c=3 are expressions, and if b and c don't exist they are created as global variables.

Now you should be able to see why:

```
var a=1,(b=2,c=3);
```

is nonsense and just generates an error, whereas:

```
var a=1,b=(2,c=3);
```

is perfectly OK and declares two local variables, a and b. What is stored in b? The answer is 3 because the expression is (2,c=3).

Using the Comma

So now we have the comma mastered - what can you use it for? The honest answer is not much. The comma is a jem but not a particularly useful one. There are places, especially in libraries, where you will find the comma operator in use, but in most cases there are much better and clearer ways of expressing the same idea. The most commonly encountered use of the comma operator is to make more complex for loops. Ideally for loops should be kept simple so making them more complex isn't something to encourage.

A JavaScript for loop has the form:

```
for(expression1;expression2;expression3)
```

The first expression is evaluated once when the loop starts and it is usually where the initialization occurs. The second expression is evaluated before each new iteration of the loop. If it evaluates to false the loop stops. The final expression is evaluated at the end of each loop iteration and it is generally where loop counters are updated.

Notice that you can write any expression you care to in a for loop and you can use the comma operator so that you can write multiple expressions. So, for example, what do you think the following is all about?

```
for(let i=0,j=10;i<=j;i++,j--){
  console.log(i*j);
}
```

The first expression isn't a use of the comma operator. It just uses the var statement to create two local variables, i and j, and sets them to 0 and 10 respectively. The second expression is a simple test for i being less than or equal to j, and doesn't use the comma operator. The final expression is the only use of the comma operator and it adds one to i and subtracts one from j each time through the loop. So the values of i and j we create are:

```
0 10
1 9
2 8
3 7
4 6
5 5
```

and then the loop ends.

Clever? You could just as easily have written the loop as:

```
for(let i=0;i<=5;i++){
 console.log(i*(10-i));
}
```

You can use a similar technique to turn a while loop into a sort of for loop:

```
var i=0;
while(i++,i<10){
 console.log(i)
}
```

There are lots of similar uses and examples, but they all come down to the same thing - we need to use a single expression, but also need to evaluate some other expressions first just for their side effects.

Relationship to Active Logic

The comma operator , can be thought of as being a member of the same family as &&, || and ? discussed in the previous jem.

To summarize:

```
expressionA || expressionB
```

evaluates expressionA - if truthy then expressionA is the result, otherwise the right-hand expression is evaluated and is the result.

```
expressionA && expressionB
```

evaluates expressionA - if falsey then expressionA is the result, otherwise the right-hand expression is evaluated and is the result.

```
expressionA ? expressionB:expressionC
```

evaluates expressionA - if truthy it evaluates expressionB as the result and otherwise it evaluates expressionC as the result.

The comma operator:

```
expressionA , expressionB
```

evaluates expressionA then the right-hand expression is evaluated and is the result.

It is also worth noting that the comma operator works well with any of the other active logic operators. In particular, the ternary operator ? can often make use of it. For example:

```
triesLeft ? (triesLeft--,try()):(noMoreTries(),Finish());
```

If you assume that triesLeft is a counter of how many attempts the user still has, you can decrement it and call the try function or call noMoreTries to inform the user that they have failed and then stop the program.

In conclusion, the situation is best summed up as "*you need to understand the comma, but you probably don't need to use it*". What really matters is that you don't confuse the many other uses of the comma with the comma operator.

Jem 10

Code As Data

"It is a bad plan that admits of no modification."
Publilius Syrus

JavaScript, being an interpreted language, can modify its own code as it runs. Self-modifying code can be dangerous, but you should know about it and how it works. If you would like to experiment, read on. This one is a jem with sharp edges.

When programming was a young subject and vacuum tubes ruled the earth, a very powerful, but very scary technique, was invented – self-modifying code. The whole beauty of the stored program computer design was that the data and program were treated in the same way. A program plus the data it needed to work with were loaded into memory and the program simply accessed and modified the data as required. This idea was so new and powerful that programmers often didn't really distinguish between the program and the data and allowed one part of the program to modify another part of the program.

Self-modifying code can effectively re-write itself as it runs and as such you can guess that it's powerful, but you should also be able to see that it creates a nightmare for debugging and generally understanding what is going on. After all, if code is self modifying, there is no simple static piece of text that can be read through to check it makes sense. You have to read the code and keep updating what the program is as it modifies itself. As a result self-modifying code not only fell out of favor, it was actively demonized as something that only really evil programming languages would allow you to do. So, if you think that self-modifying code has just been invented and is something connected with the new wave of dynamic languages, think again – it's old, but still relatively untamed.

After all of this you might be surprised to learn that JavaScript allows self-modifying code. Indeed, most interpreted or dynamic languages do.

Dynamic Functions - Function to String

The reason why JavaScript supports runtime modifiable code is that the program itself is just data stored in a variable. Consider the way you can define a function, see Jem 3 - Functions Are Objects:

```
function myfunc1(){alert("MyFunc 1");
```

which is almost exactly equivalent to:

```
myFunc1=function(){alert("MyFunc 1")};
```

The second form looks like a variable assignment, and indeed it is. If you don't believe me try:

```
alert(myFunc1);
```

and you will see the text of the function just as if it was a string. What you actually see depends on the browser, but the general principle is that you should see the text of the function. However, MyFunc1 isn't actually a string – it is a Function object. What is going on here is that the Function object's toString method is being called, see Jem 6: Objects have Value, and this returns a string representation of the function:

```
alert(myFunc1.toString());
```

Although this isn't guaranteed, it works in all the major browsers. There is also a rather more non-standard method called toSource which works in Firefox, but not in most other browsers. Also notice that you can't see the source code for internally defined functions, only user defined functions. You can take a function and convert it into a string using:

```
myString=myFunc1.toString();
alert(myString);
```

or you can use the String object's constructor and an implied call to the toString method:

```
myString=new String(myFunc1);
```

Of course, now that you have the function represented as a string you can edit it in any way that you like. For example, you can change the 1 into a 2 using:

```
myString=myString.replace("1","2");
alert(myString);
```

This changes what is stored in the string into:

```
function(){alert("MyFunc2")};
```

Notice that this is a string and there is no way you can directly execute this new function, i.e.

```
myString();
```

doesn't do anything. How to make a string back into a function is our next challenge.

The Round Trip - String to Function

The real question is how to get the string back into a function and there are a number of ways of doing this. The most direct is to use the `Function` object's constructor. If you write:

```
myFunc=new Function("arg1","arg2"…"statements");
```

the new function will be created with the specified arguments and statements. Notice that the last string passed to the constructor is taken to be the body of the new function.

To use this with our string we simply have to strip off the "`function()`" part of the string. Unfortunately some browsers place a space between "`function`" and "`()`" and some don't and this makes the task slightly harder.

You can probably improve on this simple-minded implementation of the constructor:

```
myFunc2=new Function(myString.
      replace("function()","").
            replace("function ()",""));
myFunc2();
```

The easy way out is to simply attempt to replace `function` followed by no space or followed by one space. In the real world you would use a regular expression and spend much more time getting it right. Notice that there are no parameters used in this function and writing a routine to convert any function in the form of a string into a real function using the `Function` object constructor is slightly more difficult as it involves a lot of string manipulation to get things in the correct form.

Fortunately there is an easier method based on using `eval`.

String To Function Using eval

The `eval` function accepts a string of JavaScript statements and executes them as if they were within your program.

Before you get worried because you have heard that `eval` is evil, be assured that it isn't. It is one of the more powerful features of JavaScript and many an interpreted language. As it is powerful, it is capable of misuse and if allowed to process user or server input then it can cause the program to do things you never dreamed of. However, this doesn't mean you can't use `eval` internally in a safe way.

Programmers often claim such-and-such an instruction is dangerous without saying why. In the case of `eval` the only danger is that some outside agent will feed in an expression that evaluates to something that you didn't expect, or would not have allowed had you expected it. In other words, if the string to be evaluated has its origins in any way influenced by the outside world then you have to make sure that the outside world doesn't manage to feed it a string that does something evil. You can do this by checking that the string to be evaluated is limited in some way, usually referred to as sanitizing the input, or you can simply find some less powerful way to achieve the same result, i.e. don't use eval. If, however, the string to be evaluated originates within your program and is 100% under control, what could possibly go wrong?

So to convert a string to a function you simply use:

```
myString=myString.replace("1","2");
eval("myFunc2=" + myString);
myFunc2();
```

which displays the alert box "MyFunc2". From this point on in the program myFunc2 behaves like a standard Function object. Notice that its scope is determined by the scope of the myFunc2 variable and the function only exists after the eval operation, i.e. there is no function hoisting.

This completes the "round-trip" in the sense that you can now convert a function to a string, modify it and convert it back to a function or you can simply put a function together as a string as the program runs and convert it to a function when you want to use it. This gives you the power to write self-modifying code of arbitrary complexity and the same tricks can be used to modify object methods just as easily.

Simpler Self-Modification

It is worth mentioning that some of the most useful forms of self-modification are much simpler and much safer than the general scheme outlined above. Consider the following:

```
myfunc=function(){
 if(browser=="IE") {
  alert("Browser 1");
 } else {
  alert("Browser 2");
 }
};
```

In this case myfunc has to deal with the possibility that it might be run on one of two types of browser and what it has to do is browser-specific. It does this using a simple if statement but each time the function is called the selection has to be made, even though once loaded the browser type cannot change. That is, each time myfunc is called it has to check the state of the browser variable, even though it can't have changed since the last time it was used. We can make this all much more efficient by simply redefining the function depending on which version of the browser it finds itself in:

```
myfunc=function(){
 if(browser=="IE"){
  myfunc=function() {alert("Browser 1")};
 } else {
  myfunc=function() {alert("Browser 2")};
 };
 myfunc();
};
```

Notice that the system is sophisticated enough to buffer the function definition so that changing it midway through its execution has no effect. However, the new call to the function at the end of the modification does run the new function.

If you find this confusing simply compare the function's definition before and after it has been run:

```
var browser="IE";
alert(myfunc);
myfunc();
alert(myfunc);
```

Before the first call the function is as listed above, complete with the if statement. After the first call it simply reads:

```
function() {alert("Browser 1")};
```

and no test is made to see which browser it is being run in until it is started afresh, possibly in a different browser.

The principle is based on the idea that a function is just an object and a variable can be set to reference that object. If you want to change the object that the variable is referencing you can – and this applies to functions as well as other types of object.

This is a very attractive idea. Creating self-modifying functions in this way is a safe thing to do and is used in a number of JavaScript libraries. You can use this technique to create a function that is customized to its environment. Simply test the environment on the first run and then replace the function by the custom function for subsequent uses.

What Is Self-Modification Useful For?

What else can you use self-modifying code for? In general, uses of self-modifying code are advanced. Typically they are about adding facilities to the language. For example, suppose you want to add a print command to JavaScript as a shorthand for console.log. You could scan any function for `print(`*`string`*`)` and convert it to `console.log(`*`string`*`)`. Equally you could simply redefine `console.log` as in:

```
let print=console.log;
```

A dynamic language such as JavaScript generally has multiple ways of achieving the same advanced idea.

More generally, self modifying techniques correspond to compiling code, whereas alternatives are interpreter-based approaches. To make this clear, consider implementing a Domain Specific Language for arithmetic with commands `add`, `sub`, `mul` and `div`. The code modifying approach would take a string like:

```
dsl="add(3, mul(4,5))" ;
```

and convert it, using string functions, to:

```
dsl=3+4*5;
```

and then use

```
eval(dsl);
```

to get a result.

We have converted the code into something that can be executed directly - this is what compilers do. The alternative is to process the original string and call functions to do the intended job. That is, scan the string and find `"mul(a,b)"` and call the function `mul(a,b)`. Next scan for `"add(c,d)"` and call the function `add(c,d)` and so on accumulating the result. In the case of the example expression scanning the string would result in calling:

```
add(3,mul(4,5));
```

Notice that in this case no part of the string is executed as code. Instead functions are called depending on what the string contains. This is how interpreters work.

In general you always have a choice between converting a string into executable code, i.e. compile it, or examine it and call functions depending on what it contains, i.e. interpret it.

Self-modifying code is dangerous and often over complex – use it with great care and not very often. Prefer interpreting strings to compiling them.

Jem 11

Lambda Expressions

"There may, indeed, be other applications of the system than its use as a logic."

Alonzo Church

Lambda expressions sound advanced and impressive and just about every language has them or is adding them. Put simply, lambda expressions are something of a buzz word, so much that it's difficult to know what they really are all about.

One place you won't hear much about lambda expressions is in JavaScript. You will even hear it said that JavaScript doesn't do lambdas, but this isn't the whole truth. JavaScript could always do lambda expressions, even before ES2015 introduced something equivalent to them.

First what is a lambda expression? Lambda expressions were invented by Alonzo Church and Stephen Kleene, two great computer scientists, back in the 1930s. In practice, this is fairly irrelevant in the sense that when most programmers use the term lambda expression they mean a function of a number of parameters that returns a single result and can be passed to other functions. The parameters and single result clearly aren't a problem but what about passing a function to other functions?

Functions As Objects

We have already discovered, see Jem 3, that functions are objects that have some code associated with them that you can execute using the invocation () operator. What this means in practice is that a variable can store data or code with the only real difference being that the code can be executed.

This is often summarized by saying that functions in JavaScript are "first class" objects. That is, without the help of lambda expressions you can already pass functions to other functions and use them as if they were objects.

Contrast this to what happens in many other languages where functions are something completely different from objects and are usually thought of as being constituent parts of an object, namely methods. For example, consider the original version of Java, which as you will recall, has little to do with JavaScript other than its name. In Java everything is an object, but its objects have properties that can either be data or a functions. In this way functions are treated as methods and they always belong to an object. There is no sense in which a function can exist outside of an object. In Java, if you want to pass a function to a method then your only choice is to create an object which has that function as a method and pass the entire object. This is so unwieldy that recently Java introduced lambda expressions, which makes it possible to pass a function to a method without having to include it as a method in an object.

Any language that treats functions as something different from objects usually has to introduce lambda expressions or something similar. For example, C# introduced delegates, objects that wrap functions, and more recently full lambda expressions. All very complicated and not as elegant as JavaScript's approach.

Put simply we need lambda expressions to provide us with functions that have a life of their own outside of objects and so that they can be passed around like objects.

JavaScript doesn't need lambda expressions for either of these reasons as function are already objects and have a life of their own. You might say that this jem is about the fact that JavaScript doesn't need to invent something to solve a problem it never had. Except, of course, ES2015 did just that and introduced something that looks like and behaves like a lambda function, see later.

Passing Functions

Given you can pass an object, i.e. as a parameter, into a function, it now seems entirely logical that you can pass a variable that just happens to reference a function object into another function. Recall that all parameters in JavaScript are passed by reference so just a pointer to the function is passed and this is efficient. If you don't see why you would want to pass a function then you haven't noticed that this is what you do every time you set up an event handler or a callback.

More generally, passing functions is also a fairly useful when you want to create a function that does a standard task, but with big variations. For example, the Array object has a method that will sort the array into order:

```
var list=new Array("A","AB","ABC","ABCD");
list.sort();
for(var i=0;i<list.length  ;i++){
  alert(list[i]);
}
```

What is perhaps slightly less well known is that the `sort` method can also take an optional function which it will use to compare the values of the array. This function is defined as:

```
function(a,b)
```

and it returns a negative value if a is smaller than b, zero if a is equal to b and a positive value if a is larger than b. For example:

```
compare=function(a,b){
  return a.length-b.length;
}
```

used in:

```
list.sort(compare);
```

sorts the list of strings into order based on their length alone.

Other languages that don't have first class functions have to resort to delegate types, which are object wrappers for functions - or lambda expressions. So JavaScript's functions almost do the same as a lambda but if you know about lambda functions you might object that having to first define the function and then use it in a call is less than elegant. Well, JavaScript has anonymous functions, which can be defined within the function call.

Anonymous Functions

Things are even simpler because you don't have to store a reference to a function to pass it to another function or to make use of it.

As already described, other languages have to introduce something special to allow this to happen. In JavaScript it is just a consequence of the fact that all objects are anonymous and functions are objects. There is also the principle that anywhere you can use an object reference you can use an object literal. You could say that this is a mini-jem and while it isn't generally useful it is worth knowing about. For example, instead of writing:

```
var list=new Array("A","AB","ABC","ABCD");
list.sort();
```

you can use:

```
var result=["A","AB","ABC","ABCD"].sort();
```

Anywhere you can use a variable that is a reference to an object you can use an object literal.

JavaScript supports anonymous functions as object literals and you can write this example as:

```
list.sort(function(a,b){
    return a.length-b.length;
});
```

The only real problem with this is how to format the line using indents that show where the function literal starts and ends. The indent shown above is one used by some automatic JavaScript formatters. An alternative solution is:

```
list.sort(
  function(a,b){
    return a.length-b.length;
  }
);
```

which makes matching brackets slightly easier.

For short functions a single line also works:

```
list.sort(function(a,b){return a.length-b.length;});
```

This last example looks a lot like the typical way that lambda expressions are used in other languages. In C# you could write the same thing using:

```
list.sort((a,b) => a.length-b.length)
```

and the expression:

```
(a,b) => a.length-b.length
```

is a lambda expression.

Notice that apart from being a little more compact - no need for the keywords function and return - it is more or less the same as a JavaScript anonymous function. Thus JavaScript, with its first class functions or functions as objects, doesn't really need lambda expressions or it already has them depending on your point of view.

The Arrow Function

JavaScript doesn't really need anything like a lambda expression, but that didn't stop one being added in ES2015 – the arrow function. While the arrow function isn't strictly necessary, it does make JavaScript look more like languages which do have lambda expressions.

The arrow function is mostly a condensed syntax for the function expression. You can use it to define a function as simply as:

```
(param1,param2,…,paramn)=> {statements};
```

For example:

```
(a,b)=>{
        var ans=a+b;
        return ans;
      };
```

returns a Function object which can be used in the normal way.

You can store a reference to the arrow function in a variable:

```
var myFunction=(a,b)=>{
                    var ans=a+b;
                    return ans;
                  };
```

and you can call the function in the usual way:

```
myFunction(1,2);
```

You can use arrow functions as literals. So the previous example involving sort can be written:

```
list.sort((a,b)=>{return a.length-b.length;});
```

You can see that this really does look like what other languages call a lambda expression.

There are some syntactic shortcuts you can use that make arrow functions look even more like lambdas and make them even harder to read. For example, you don't have to use a return. If you write a single expression then its value is automatically returned:

```
list.sort((a,b)=> a.length-b.length);
```

Notice that the expression isn't within {} and you can only have a single expression.

You can also omit the parentheses if the arrow function has only a single parameter. For example:

```
a => a.length;
```

is a function that returns the length of a.

Finally an arrow function with no parameters has to use a pair of empty parentheses:

```
()=>{alert("Hello World")};
```

This is more or less all there is to an arrow function – with one exception. Arrow functions do not have a this of their own, they inherit whatever value for this is in use at the time of their declaration. This makes them less suitable for use as method definitions, but much better for passing to other functions as parameters. Otherwise everything that is true of a function expression is also true of an arrow function. In particular you can use rest parameters, default parameters and destructuring just as you can in a standard function. The only substantial difference, apart from the syntax, is the aforementioned way this is treated

Accidental Invocation

Is there a downside to having functions as objects? Perhaps the only real problem is the potential confusion between the object and the function or, more exactly, between the function and its invocation. You can create your own functions that accept other functions, but you have to be careful exactly how you do it and how you make use of them. For example:

```
Say=function(t){
      t();
    }
```

will simply call any function that you pass to it. If you define:

```
Hello=function(){
  alert("Hello");
}
```

then:

```
Say(Hello);
```

will call the Hello function and display an alert.

Notice that you have to pass the variable that references the function without accidentally invoking the function. That is, don't write:

```
Say(Hello());
```

by mistake as this would call the Hello function and then pass its result to the Say function which, as it is a string, couldn't be called as a function. Similarly, including parentheses in the parameter list in the definition of the function would be a syntax error.

You need to distinguish very clearly between passing a function object and passing the result of a function to another function. This problem doesn't occur in languages that restrict functions to being methods of objects. You then pass an object and you don't think of trying to invoke it because it is an object not a function.

Immediate Invocation ( )

You need to get into the habit of thinking of the round brackets () as being the function invocation operator. Whenever you use () following an expression it calls the function that is the result of the expression. For example, you can write:

```
Say=function(t){
  t();
}(Hello);
```

and the round brackets at the end of the function definition call the function as soon as it has been defined. This is usually called an "Immediately Invoked Function Expression" or IIFE and is very useful and used a lot in idiomatic JavaScript in connection with anonymous function and arrow functions.

This instant function evaluation can be useful when you want to pass the result of a "lambda expression", for example:

```
alert(function(a,b){return a+b;}(1,2));
```

or:

```
alert(((a,b)=>{return a+b;})(1,2));
```

Here we have a lambda expression, a sum function, being defined and evaluated in a single step. The result, 3 in this case, is passed to the `alert` function.

Although this example isn't particularly useful it does become useful when combined with other JavaScript features such as closure. For example, suppose we have a function that needs to access a private variable:

```
var myPrivate=0;
function myFunction(){
        myPrivate++;
        return myPrivate;
    }
```

The variable might be called `myPrivate`, but it is accessible from any other code that can call `myFunction`. To make it really private you have to wrap it in another function and immediately invoke it:

```
 var myFunction = (function () {
                  var myPrivate = 0;
                  return function () {
                          myPrivate++;
                          return myPrivate;
                      };
              })();
```

This looks complicated, but you can see that the outer anonymous function returns a reference to:

```
function () {
            myPrivate++;
            return myPrivate;
        };
```

which is the previous function, but now `myPrivate` is in its execution context and hence part of the closure. The outer function is immediately executed with the sole idea of creating the closure. Enclosing a function within another function and using immediate execution is an idiomatic way of creating private resources via closure.

The introduction of arrow functions to provide lambdas is is an odd jem because it tackles a problem JavaScript had already solved and appears to be an addition just to "keep up" with the other languages. Arrow functions don't make JavaScript worse, and they can be more expressive, but overuse can make code look cryptic. They could be used in many of the examples in this book, but functions or anonymous functions are preferred because they look easier.

Fluent Interfaces

"Our business in living is to become fluent with the life we are living, and art can help this."
John Cage

One of JavaScript's attractive features is the way that you can build up chains of commands that look almost like the way you would use a language. This is more generally called a "Fluent Interface" and it isn't difficult to implement.

The idea of a fluent interface was first coined by Eric Evans and Martin Fowler to express the idea of an object-oriented API. The technique uses method chaining, but if you want to call it a fluent interface it also has to have the characteristics of a DSL, Domain Specific Language. Put simply, the way that the methods chain together has to express natural sets of operations. Ideally the chains of methods should read as if you were writing a tiny program with verbs and modifiers.

First let's take a look at the mechanism of chaining. In what follows don't worry too much about why you would want to do things. Concentrate instead on how they work. The advantages of chaining and fluent interfaces will become clear later.

General Chaining

Chaining is where you call one function after another. For example:

```
function1().function2().function3()
```

and so on. It is usual, but not necessary, for the first function to be a method belonging to a particular object:

```
myObject.function1().function2().function3()
```

and so on.

The object version of the chaining is the common idiom in other languages where functions aren't first class objects. In JavaScript, however, functions are first class objects, see Jem 3: Functions Are Objects, and this makes the first form of chaining perfectly reasonable.

127

When you first see something like this, you can't help but wonder why it all works. Indeed, it doesn't work unless you arrange for the functions to fit together.

The principle of chaining is that each function has to return an object, which supports the next function in the chain as a method.

This is all there is to function chaining. It's simple, but it is easy to become confused in real cases. Take, for example, the chain:

```
function1().function2().function3()
```

For this to work function1 has to return an object which has function2 as a method. For simplicity, suppose obj2 has function2 as a method and obj3 has function3 as a method. First we need to define function1:

```
function1 = function(){
                alert("function 1");
                return obj2;
            }
```

As promised, this returns obj2 which is defined as:

```
var obj2 = {
         function2: function () {
                    alert("function 2");
                    return  obj3;
         }
    };
```

which, again as promised, returns obj3 which is defined as:

```
var obj3 = {
         function3: function () {
                    alert("function 3");
                    return obj3;
         }
    };
```

With these definitions you can now write:

```
function1().function2().function3();
```

and when you run the program you will see three alert boxes announcing three functions in turn. Of course, in practice the functions could have parameters and the objects could be generated by constructor functions requiring that we use new to create a new instance of each object to return.

Notice that it is the object returned by each function that gives the next function in the chain its context. That is, you can determine exactly what function is called by the object you return, so not only is this set to the object you have returned, but the function that is used depends on the object you return. For example, if the function was a search operation, then the display function called next could be automatically varied according to the type of object returned by the search. That is you call `.display` but the function you get depends on the object returned. This is a sort of natural polymorphism that all dynamically-typed languages have. Also notice that if you define `function1` as a method of `obj1` then this works, but now you have to start the chain with `obj1`:

```
obj1.function1().function2().function3();
```

This is all there is to function chaining and it all depends on each function returning an object which has the next function among its methods. However, this isn't the most common way that function chaining is used.

Singleton Chaining

Before we get on to more complicated examples, let's examine another simple case - singleton chaining. A singleton is a JavaScript object that isn't created by a constructor - it is an object literal. In this case what we want to do is allow each function to be defined as a method of the same object, `obj` say.

To allow chaining we have to arrange for each method to return an object that each subsequent function is defined on and in this case it is just `obj`. It really is this simple. So let's define our object with three methods:

```
var obj = {
        function1: function () {
            alert("function1");
            return obj;
        },
        function2: function () {
            alert("function2");
            return obj;
        },
        function3: function () {
            alert("function3");
            return obj;
        }
    }
```

Notice that each function returns a reference to `obj` and this is what allows the next function call in the chain to work. With this definition you can write:

```
obj.function1().function2().function3();
```

and you will see the three alert boxes indicating that each function is called in turn.

Notice that this all depends on the variable `obj` not being reassigned between function calls. If you want to protect against this you need to create a private variable using closure that cannot be changed that the functions can return, or you can use a `const` if you are using ES2015.

Creating a private variable using closure is fairly easy:

```
var obj = function () {
        self = {
            function1: function () {
                        alert("function1");
                        return self;
            },
            function2: function () {
                        alert("function2");
                        return self;
            },
            function3: function () {
                        alert("function3");
                        return self;
            }
        };
        return self;
    }();
```

Notice that what has happened is that we have wrapped the object definition in a function. This forces the self variable into the closure and all of the functions defined can access it, but no other part of the code can. Also notice that use of an immediate invocation of the function as explained at the end of the previous jem.

Instance Chaining

Singletons can be very useful, but often we want to be able to create as many instances of an object as desired and in this case we have to move on to look at instance chaining. This is very similar to the singleton case, but now we have to create a constructor that will produce an instance of the object.

```
var objConstruct = function(){
        this.function1= function () {
            alert("function1");
            return this;
        };
        this.function2=function () {
            alert("function2");
            return this;
        };
        this.function3= function () {
            alert("function3");
            return this;
        }
    };
```

Notice that we have defined three methods for the object we are constructing, but also notice the use of this to reference the object being constructed. What should each of the functions return to ensure that the next function can be called? In this case each function has to return `this` because, when the function is called, `this` references the instance that the function is a method of. Now we can write:

```
var obj = new objConstruct();
obj.function1().function2().function3();
```

and again we see the alert boxes announce that each function is called in turn.

If you can't see the difference between this and the singleton example, remember that we can now create as many instances of the object as we like. Also notice that because each function returns `this` as the object for the next function, all of the functions in the chain are called in the context of the same instance of the object.

Optional Chaining

ES2020 introduced the optional chaining operator `?.` which can be used to handle potential errors in fluent calls. The idea is very simple:

```
object?.property
```

will return `undefined` if `object` is nullish, i.e. `null` or `undefined`, and the specified property otherwise. Notice that this is also a short circuit evaluation in that the property is not evaluated if `object` is nullish. Using optional chaining isn't difficult, but you do have to think about exactly what you are testing. For example:

```
A={};
A.method1=function(){console.log("method1");};
A?.method1();
```

works perfectly and you see `method1` displayed as `A` is not nullish. However, if you try:

```
A?.method2();
```

you will see a runtime error because `A` is defined and hence an attempt is made to retrieve `method2` and then call it. If `method2` doesn't exist then a runtime error is generated. If `method2` exists but isn't a function a runtime error is generated. To protect against `method2` not being defined you need to use:

```
A?.method2?.();
```

or

```
A.method2?.();
```

Notice that you will still get a runtime error if `method2` is defined but not a function. This is a slight extension of the optional chaining notation, but perfectly reasonable in that the invocation operator `()` is only evaluated if `A.method2` is defined.

If you try:

```
let B;
let C=B?.method2();
```

you will discover that `C` is undefined and no runtime error occurs. Notice however, if `B` is undeclared, i.e. no `let B`, then you will still get a runtime error.

The more general form:

```
object?.expression
```

can be used with any form of expression that makes sense in the context of accessing a property.

For example:

```
let result=myArray?.[42];
```

will return `undefined` if `myArray` is nullish and:

```
let result=myObject?.[propName];
```

will also return `undefined` if `myArray` is nullish.

Finally, it is worth noting that you cannot use optional chaining on the left-hand side of an assignment.

Getting Complicated

Once again, this is all there is to chaining - just make sure you return the correct object for the next function to have the correct context. If you want to be sophisticated then you don't always have to return the same object and, as already mentioned, this would be appropriate for a search method, say, that returned different types of object.

One problem with chained function calls is what do you do about the result of a function? After all, you can't return it because to support chaining you have to return a suitable object. The answer is that the object you return has to be both the context for the next function call and incorporate the result of the function.

That is, if you want to implement an API in a fluent style then you have to create an object which not only hosts the methods you want to chain, but which stores what would have been the results of these operations as its internal state. Let's take a look at some examples.

Initialization

One common use of function chaining is to create a fluent interface to initialize an object. You can initialize everything using the constructor, but this often results in a constructor that is very difficult to use. Providing set functions that can be chained produces a neater and more flexible initialization API. For example, suppose you have an address object which holds a person's details, then you could define the constructor as:

```
var AddressConstruct = function () {
        this.name;
        this.number;
        this.age;
        this.setName = function (name) {
            this.name = name;
            return this;
        };
        this.setNumber = function (number){
            this.number = number;
            return this;
        };
        this.setAge = function (age) {
            this.age = age;
            return this;
        }
    };
```

Following this definition you can write things like:

```
var add = new AddressConstruct();
add.setAge(24).setName("Ian").setNumber(1);
```

Once you have seen the basic method you can see that it is possible to extend the idea to include methods to modify values that have already been set. For example, you could have an addAge method which increments the age field and so on.

A DSL For Calculation

As an example of how function chaining can become a DSL, Domain Specific Language, consider the task of implementing a calculator or math API. JavaScript already has the Math object, which provides many standard functions, but this is an example of how it could have been done.

The first problem we have to solve is that, unlike a non-fluent approach to calculation, our functions cannot return the result of the calculation. In fact, the result has to be stored as the state of the calc object. This is another common pattern in using function chaining - what used to be a result often has to be built into the object's state.

The constructor is:

```
var CalcConstruct = function () {
    this.value = 0;
    this.square = function () {
     this.value = Math.pow(this.value, 2);
     return this;
    };
    this.sqrt = function () {
     this.value = Math.sqrt(this.value);
     return this;
    };
    this.display = function () {
     alert(this.value);
     return this;
    };
    this.setValue = function (value) {
     this.value = value;
     return this;
    };
    this.times = function (times) {
     this.value = this.value * times;
     return this;
    };
  };
```

Notice that all of the functions work with `this.value` and return `this`.

The range of operations is quite small - `square`, `sqrt`, `times`, `setValue` and `display`. Even so, you can now write calculations that look fairly impressive, for example:

```
var c = new CalcConstruct();
  c.setValue(100)
   .sqrt()
   .display()
   .square()
   .display()
   .times(3)
   .display();
```

You can see that it does start to look like a program in a special language.

134

This final example is a little more realistic, but it hardly starts to dig into the sophistication you can invent - and JavaScript is ideal for this sort of elaboration. For example, if you make the internal state of the object a collection, you can introduce functions which select and even enumerate on the collection. You can arrange for functions to return different types of object to implement conditionals and so on. You can also pass functions within methods to determine what happens.

For example:

```
c.apply(sin).reduce(sum);
```

could be implemented to apply the sin function to each member of the collection and then perform a reduction on the collection using the sum function, i.e. form a total of the values in the collection.

If you want to see more examples of using the fluent style then see jQuery or LINQ both of which take function chaining as key design principles.

Jem 13

Hoisting, Scope And Lifetime

"It is necessary for him who lays out a state and arranges laws for it to presuppose that all men are evil and that they are always going to act according to the wickedness of their spirits whenever they have free scope."

Niccolo Machiavelli

This jem is usually offered up as proof that JavaScript is a crazy language. Even the name of the feature, "hoisting", sounds like a joke. However, far from being a joke, hoisting is a neat feature that lets you write code in a more natural way.

Hoisting is a JavaScript feature that allows you to make forward references to functions and variables, that is references to things that haven't yet been defined.

JavaScript has some language features that confuse beginners and experts in other languages alike, but it is often the case that the simple principle that lies behind the behavior just isn't explained. When it is, it not only seems logical but simple and the only way to do the job. So it is with "hoisting", a seemingly elaborate and complex piece of behavior that just seems to complicate things without any benefits.

First let's take a quick look at the problem that hoisting is intended to solve.

Forward References

In most programming language you use functions or procedures to break the program down into small manageable chunks. One small problem that is often not mentioned is the forward reference. Suppose you want to use a function:

```
myFunction();
```

but this isn't defined until later in the program's text. Should the program fail because myFunction isn't defined, or should the language allow you to use functions that are defined later in the text?

This is a basic distinction between the order of the text of a program and the order of execution and understanding this is one of the differences between a programmer and a non-programmer.

Early programming languages insisted that you declare everything at the start of the program. This solved the forward reference problem because all functions, and variables for that matter, were defined before the main program started and hence there was no possibility of a forward reference. On the other hand, it had the disadvantage of forcing the programmer to put all the functions first and the main program last. This bottom up approach doesn't fit naturally with the top down way we read a program, i.e. main program first.

Later, and more programmer-friendly, languages were less strict about where you should declare things. They allowed you to put function definitions anywhere within the text of the program and use them anywhere, including before they were actually defined. The way that this usually works is that the compiler or language runtime "reads" the entire program file once just to find out what functions and variables you have used. Only after this first pre-run scan does the actual program execution start, safe in knowledge that all global variables and functions are defined. This is what JavaScript does and it is the origin of the idea we usually call "hoisting".

JavaScript Forward References

JavaScript doesn't insist that you declare variables, it allows you to define functions anywhere you like and it allows you to use a function before its definition. It does this by implementing "hoisting", a picturesque term inspired by the image of the declarations being yanked up to the top of their scope.

The rule is quite simple and it makes sense to state what it is and then explore some of its consequences.

+ Hoisting moves all function declarations to the start of the function that contains them.

or

+ Hoisting moves all function declarations to the start of their enclosing scope.

As scope in JavaScript is defined by functions, the two definitions are the same.

If the declarations are not within a function then they are moved to the start of the main program, which is the scope in this case. In other words, JavaScript could have insisted that you define everything you are going to use at the start of the function that you use them in. Instead it automatically gathers things up and moves them to the correct position. Of course, it doesn't actually modify your program - but your program is run as if the declarations were at the start of the function.

The only complication is what exactly is a declaration in JavaScript? The answer is any statement that doesn't actually get executed when the program runs. A declaration simply tells the program "compiler" or runtime something useful.

In modern JavaScript there are five types of declaration:

`var, let, const, function` and `class`.

All of these are hoisted, but the effect of this can be very different.
As `function` is the declaration that hoisting was introduced to deal with, let's look at it first.

Function Declarations

A function definition or declaration doesn't involve actually carrying out any operations - you are simply defining the function so that it can be invoked later.

For example, if you write:

```
function myFunction(){
   instructions;
}
```

this doesn't actually execute the function or do anything in your program. The text of the function is simple a definition or declaration of what the function `myFunction` is.

The function is executed when it is invoked using the usual parentheses notation, so:

```
myFunction();
```

actually executes the function.

By the rule of hoisting then any function definition should be moved to the start of the function that contains it. This means that:

```
myFunction();

function myFunction(){
 alert("myfunction called");
}
```

works perfectly, even though `myFunction` is defined later in the program than where it is used.

Hoisting causes the program to be treated as if it had been written as:

```
function myFunction(){
 alert("myfunction called");
}
```

```
myFunction();
```

That is, as if the function definition had been written at the start of the program.

As previously stated, hoisting gathers all your function definitions and moves them to the top of their scope - the main program or the function that they are declared in.

Variable Declarations – var, let & const

Function declarations and hoisting is a simple idea compared to the complications of variable declarations – this is because JavaScript provides too many exceptions to a simple general rule.

When you declare a variable there are two important things about it.

The first is when the variable comes into existence and when it is destroyed and hence removed from the program. This is generally referred to as the variable's lifetime.

The second is where the variable can be accessed from within the program. This is generally referred to as the variable's scope.

JavaScript used to only support one type of scope – function scope. It now also supports a useful alternative – block scope.

- ◆ Function scope is what you might expect. The declared entity is valid within the entire function it is declared in and within any functions that are declared within the same scope.

- ◆ Block scope means that the declared entity is valid within the entire block it is declared in and from within any blocks contained within that block.

The original JavaScript declarations, i.e. `function` and `var`, have function-wide scope. The more recent additions, i.e. `let`, `const` and `class` have block-wide scope.

To summarize:

- ◆ `function` and `var` declare a function-scoped variable
- ◆ `let`, `const` and `class` declare block-scoped variables

The only real question is what is a block? Put simply, a block is defined by a pair of curly brackets {}.

For example:

```
{
   let a;
}
alert(a);
```

In this case a is declared within a block and it does not exist outside of the block and hence you will see an error that a is not defined. You can think of this as a being "local" to the block. Notice that most control structures, for, if, else, switch, while and so on are blocks and let can be used to limit the scope of variables declared within them. For example:

```
for {let i=0;i<10;i++}
```

declares a variable that is local to the for loop. Notice that you can consider a function as being a block as it has enclosing curly brackets. This means that a variable declared using let within a function has the same scope as it if had been declared using var.

Another difference between var and let is that var allows you to declare a variable more than once within the same scope but let will throw an error if you declare the same variable in the same scope. Notice that local variables, be they local to a function or a block, - always hide any identically named variables in any enclosing blocks or functions. That is JavaScript scope is hierarchical.

For example:

```
 var a=0;
 {
   let a=42;
   alert(a);
 }
 alert(a);
```

displays 42 followed by 0. In this case it doesn't make any difference if the outer variable is declared using var or let.

In JavaScript a variable can be undeclared or undefined and these two states are treated differently.

To be clear:

◆ Undeclared means that the variable doesn't yet exist and cannot be referenced

◆ Undefined means that the variable exists and can be assigned to but it doesn't have a value

See Jem 7 for more information on primitive types.

Undeclared Globals

It would be more logical if JavaScript demanded that every variable was declared, but to make it easier for beginners you can use a variable without declaring it. If you do this it is as if the variable was declared as global, i.e. at the top level of the program. That is:

```
a=0;
```

creates a global variable no matter where it is within your program unless a is declared in the same scope as the assignment. For example:

```
var a;
a=0;
```

does not declare a global variable if you are in a function. Re-declaring a variable using var in the same scope doesn't alter its value and isn't an error.

Variables that are used without being declared are very different. They are true dynamic variables created the first time they are used and global to the entire program. They also can be removed from the program using the delete operator. For example:

```
a=10;
alert(a);
delete a;
alert(a);
```

creates a global variable and displays its value, then it deletes it and the alert fails with a reference error as a no longer exists. You cannot delete a if it has been explicitly declared. The reason is that var creates a non-configurable property on the global object and this results in delete not being able to change it. Variables created using let and const can't be deleted because they don't create properties on the global object.

Hoisting Variables

A variable declared using var, let, const or class is always hoisted to the top of its scope, i.e. the function that contains it, but var behaves very differently to the others because of the way its initialization is performed. Consider:

```
function hoist(){
    a=42;
    var a;
}
hoist();
alert(a);
```

Does this create a global variable called a?

A first look suggests it should, because a is used without being declared and so it should be global, but the answer is no, because the declaration is hoisted and the program is equivalent to:

```
function hoist(){
    var a;
    a=42;
}
hoist();
alert(a);
```

If you remove the declaration then a global variable is created. If you try to retrieve a value from a variable hoisted by a `var` declaration then you will get `undefined`.

If you try this with `let` you will find that it doesn't work. The reason is that `let`, `const` and `class` are hoisted, but they have an additional rule applied. The hoisted variable is hoisted to the start of the scope, but you cannot access the variable until the declaration has been executed. This is subtle and it seems to make hoisting a waste of time as you cannot use the variable until the declaration is reached. This is not about the position of the declaration relative to the access in the code, but the order of execution. The JavaScript engine has to have encountered the declaration before you can access the variable. That is:

```
function hoist(){
    a=42;
    let a;
}

hoist();
alert(a);
```

generates an error:

```
Uncaught Reference Error: Cannot access 'a' before initialization
```

This sort of error message doesn't make much sense as a=42 is initializing the variable.

The key idea is that you cannot access the hoisted variable until after the declaration has been reached. At this point you can ask what is the point of hoisting if the program behaves as if the declaration hasn't been hoisted? The answer is that hoisting means that the JavaScript engine has registered the fact that the variable exists and is in scope and this means that any other variables that would be in scope are shadowed by the local variable.

Consider, for example:

```
function hoist(){
    a=42;
    let a;
}

var a=43;
hoist();
alert(a);
```

This looks as if the first access to a in the function should reference the global variable a, but it doesn't. You get the same error message as before because the let has been hoisted and a refers to the local variable, but the declaration has not been encountered before the assignment.

The idea is that, while all declarations are hoisted for let, const and class, you cannot access the variable until after the declaration has been reached. You can think of this as protecting you from using variables that the local declaration would have shadowed if you had put the declaration at the top of the scope. Put more directly, it stops you from creating or accessing global variables of the same name. This is generally called "the temporal dead zone" although this isn't the official title for the behavior and I don't think that the name helps understand what is going on. It is usually explained as "let, const and class variables are not initialized" and you should now be able to see that this is only a partial explanation as the prohibition on accessing the variable is on reading and writing its value.

Hoisting Recap

With the introduction of let, const and class hoisting has become something of a mess, so let's summarize:

- Hoisting makes the program behave as if all declarations, var, let, const, class and function were moved to the top of the appropriate scope.
- A var declaration initializes the variable from the start of the function scope to undefined. The variable can be accessed from the start of the scope.
- A let, const or class declaration does not initialize the variable and prohibits any access to it until the declaration is reached in the program.

This is the basic idea and it is very simple, but there are some subtle points we still need to consider.

Initialization

As well as declaring a variable, you can also initialize it in the same instruction and for a `const` declaration you have to initialize it.

For example all of:

```
var myVariable=10;
let myVariable=10;
const myVariable=10;
```

declare `myVariable` and initialize it to `10`.

By the hosting rules each of these is hoisted to the top of their respective scopes, but the initializations are left where they are. For example, the `var` declaration is equivalent to:

```
var myVariable = undefined;
    ...
myVariable=10;
```

where the `var` is moved to the top of the scope and the initialization is left exactly where you wrote it.

Notice that a `var` declaration sets the variable to undefined, but `let` and `const` don't initialize the variable. That is, the `let` declaration is equivalent to:

```
let myVariable;
    ...
myVariable=10;
```

and any attempt to make use of the variable before the original initialization results in an error.

That is, declarations with assignment hoist the declaration, but not the assignment.

Anonymous Functions

Now we reach the most commonly encountered problem with hoisting - anonymous functions.

As explained in Jem 3: Functions Are Objects, you can create anonymous functions which can either be executed at once or assigned to a variable. As an assignment is an executable statement, it shouldn't be moved and hence it shouldn't be hoisted - and there is no sensible way the function declaration can be hoisted without moving the assignment as well.

This means that anonymous functions should not be hoisted.

Consider:

```
myFunction();
var myFunction= function(){ };
```

The variable declaration `myFunction` is hoisted so when we try to call `myFunction` the variable is declared, but its value is undefined because the assignment isn't hoisted. This surprises beginners because they have grown accustomed to function declaration being hoisted along with the function definition.

If you use a `let` rather than a `var`:

```
myFunction();
let myFunction= function(){ };
```

then you get an error message about using the variable before it has been initialized.

This is the reason why you can use a named function before it is defined, but an anonymous function has to be defined before it can be used.

An anonymous function is treated differently by JavaScript - it is more a function expression than a function declaration.

Best Practice

Hoisting was introduced to allow you to forward reference functions and to a lesser extent variables. However, the best advice for avoiding difficulties with hoisting is to actually do the job manually. Always declare variables at the start of the main program or function or block, initializing if and where necessary.

Should you use `let` or `var`?

If you want to impose block scope then use `let`. If function scope would do, most programmers would still advise the use of `let` because it protects you against accidentally using variables that are already in scope.

As to functions?

If you are using function declarations then define them in an order that is logical for the understanding of the program. If you are using anonymous functions then you have to take account of where they are used and where they are defined. There seems to be no way of simplifying this and you just have to take into account that you can't forward reference an anonymous function.

To state the final position:

- Hoisting moves all declarations to the start of their enclosing scope.

- Implicit variable declarations are not hoisted.

- Declarations in JavaScript are function declarations and variable declarations need `var`, `let`, `const` and `class`.

- Function declarations are always hoisted in their entirety and hence can always be referenced before they are defined.

- An anonymous function is assigned to a variable and the declaration is hoisted, but its initialization remains put and hence cannot be referenced before it is defined.

- Explicit variable declarations are hoisted to the top of the current scope and variables declared using `var` are initialized to undefined, but variables declared using `let`, `const` or `class` are not initialized and are inaccessible until the original declaration is reached.

- An explicit declaration with assignment hoists the declaration, but not the assignment.

While this initially seems like a lot to remember it quickly becomes automatic to use `const` for all declarations unless there is a reason not to.

Amazing Async

"I do love email. Wherever possible I try to communicate asynchronously. I'm really good at email."

Elon Musk

JavaScript is really good at asynchronous. It was fairly good from the start, but with ES2015, it got so much better. This is a real jem - all shine and no flaws. The problem is that async is subtly difficult and JavaScript makes it so easy that it can be difficult to see that it really is a marvel compared to the way other languages do the job.

Async Versus Sync

The first question to answer is what is asynchronous code?

This is most easily answered by explaining what synchronous code is. In "normal" programming we write code that we expect to be executed in a specific and well-determined order. In particular, the order that code runs in is determined by the text of the program. Now compare this to event-driven asynchronous code. Event handlers are called when the user clicks on buttons, or interacts in other ways, and the order that event handlers are called isn't determined by the code, but by the outside world.

- ◆ Synchronous code executes in a well defined predetermined order.
- ◆ Asynchronous code executes in an order determined by external factors.

In the real world things are not quite as simple and asynchronous code may be used for other reasons. For example, if you want to download a file then you can do this using synchronous code:

```
download file
wait for file to download
process file
```

However, it might be better to treat the download as if is was an asynchronous operation and set a function to be run when the download is complete

```
download file call processFile when download is complete
get on with other tasks
```

You could say that asynchronous code results when you cannot afford to wait for an operation to complete. In such a case you convert the synchronous code to a function that is called when the operation completes - a callback function. You can also think of the callback as an event handler that handles the event that the operation is complete.

Notice that asynchronous code always implies some degree of parallelism in the sense that the computer has to be capable of doing something else instead of simply waiting. For example, if the computer cannot run some other process while waiting for a file to download, then it might as well wait for the file to download. However, the degree of parallelism varies from being virtually none, in the sense that there is just a single thread of execution, to being fully parallel, with multiple processors and cores working on the job.

Asynchronous computing is a complicated thing to define, but you generally know it when you see it.

Run To Completion

The basic philosophy of JavaScript's approach to asynchronous is very simple. It minimizes the programmer's exposure to the complexities of parallel programming by implementing a "run-to-completion" principle. Other languages don't always do this and they are arguably harder to work with. The run-to-completion idea is very simple - any code that starts running runs until it is complete. If this seems obvious to you then you have never used a language that allows "preemption". Many languages permit the operating system to interrupt code at any time, do something else, and then restart the code from the place it was interrupted.

You might at first think that this is perfectly reasonable and nothing can go wrong, but this ignores any possible changes in state in the wider system. Suppose you have a function which prints 0 to 9 on the console written in a language that permits preemption. Then the function could be interrupted at any point in the sequence and another process might print something, so breaking up the list of numbers. Each time you run the function it would be interrupted at a random point and so what you would see would vary. This is a simple example of a race condition where what happens depends on the order in which processes run.

If you consider the same problem in a language that doesn't allow preemption and applies the run-to-completion principle then the behavior is much simpler. In this case when the function that prints 0 to 9 starts, it will not be interrupted and so you always see 0 to 9 printed. What happens before and after the function has been called might change, but what the function does is fixed. This is the advantage of the principle. It doesn't eliminate race conditions, but it minimizes them and makes it easier to predict what code actually does.

The Event Queue

Many JavaScript programmers don't make use of the fact that JavaScript code is non-preemptable when thinking about their programs. For example, when JavaScript is loaded the code consists of function definitions, which are stored, and code outside of function definitions, which is executed to its completion without interruption.

What this means is that, even if there are events pending and event handlers set up ready to respond, no event handler will be called until the main program has run to completion. This means that, until the main program comes to an end, the user interface (UI) appears to be frozen and unresponsive. In other words, your main program's task is to set things up and get out of the way as quickly as possible. Its sole purpose in life is to set up the event handlers that do the real work. This is not how most programmers using other languages think about things.

The same argument applies to any function – that is, all functions are run to completion and are not interrupted. This means that once an event handler starts running it cannot be interrupted by another event and again, as long as it is running, the UI seems frozen.

It is clear that if code always runs to completion there has to be some way of keeping events so that they can be serviced once the current code is completed. This results in the idea of an event dispatch queue. When an event occurs it doesn't cause the associated event handler to be called at once. Instead a record is created and stored in a first-in-first-out (FIFO) queue. When the currently executing code comes to an end, the thread of execution turns its attention to the event queue and takes a record from the front of the queue and starts its event handler running. When this has completed, the thread returns to the queue and takes the next event record and continues like this until the program ends. If the event queue is empty the thread simply waits for an event record to become available.

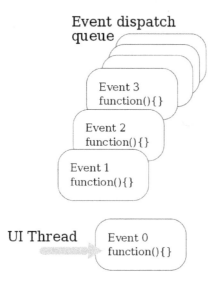

Event dispatch queue

Event 3
function(){}

Event 2
function(){}

Event 1
function(){}

UI Thread

Event 0
function(){}

You can see that for this to work each event handler has to complete quickly and free the thread to process the next event. Big complicated event handlers cause the UI to appear sluggish, or at worst frozen. This is the disadvantage of the non-preemptable code approach - each function has to be short and fast. If code is preemptable then events could be arranged to interrupt long-running code to keep the UI responsive. The sole advantage of using an event queue and non-preemptable code is that it is easier to see what is happening. Things always happen in a predictable order - events are serviced in the order in which they happen and each event handler completes before the next one starts.

Moving away from events, most long-running actions make use of a callback to signal that they are complete. Although we make a distinction between callbacks and events, they work in the same way. The only real difference is that an event handler is called when an external event occurs and a callback responds to an event, such as downloading a file, that has been initiated by the code. Callbacks are also placed in the event queue and processed in the same way as what you might think of as true event handlers.

Notice that simply using a function as an argument in a function doesn't make it a callback - it's just a first class function being used in a higher order function, see Jem 16: Functional and Not Quite Functional. To be a callback it also has to be placed in, and processed by, the event queue and hence used after the code that created it has completed.

For example in:

```
const myArray = ["a", "b", "c"];
const myArray2 = myArray.map(function (element) {
                                return element.toUpperCase();
                            }
                        );
```

the function that is passed to the map method isn't a callback as it is simply used within `map` - it is called while `map` is still running.

However, in:

```
setTimeout(function(){do something},0);
```

`function` is a callback because it is placed in the event queue and it is called after the code that `setTimeout` is in has finished running.

Many programmers refer to any use of a function as an argument to another function call as a "callback" which isn't quite correct.

Sequencing

If you restrict your attention to events then there is no problem in using callbacks or event handlers to do the job. Once you allow your code to start asynchronous processes, and hence need to use callbacks in this context, things become more difficult. The reason is sequencing.

For example, a typical task is to load an image:

```
function getImage(imageUTL,callback){
 var img = new Image();
 img.addEventListener('load', callback, false);
 img.src = imageURL;
}
```

If you want to load two images you can just write:

```
getImage(url1,callback1);
getImage(url2,callback2);
```

This works perfectly and the image loading is overlapped and which image loads first depends on external factors. The callbacks are only called after all of the code has completed. This looks sequential, but it isn't. Both `callback1` and `callback2` are executed after the code that `getImage` calls is completed and the order in which they are executed depends on which image loads first.

Suppose you only want to load the second image if the first one fails. You can't write something like:

```
if(getImage(url1,callback1)===fail) getImage(url2,callback2);
```

because `callback1` is called after all of the current code has finished and so the `if` statement has completed before we know whether the image load has worked or not.

If you want this to be sequential you have to write something like:

```
getImage(url1,function(){
              if(fail) getImage(url2,callback2)
              ...
              }
       );
```

This is the start of what has come to be known as callback hell or the callback pyramid. You have to keep including callbacks within callbacks to achieve a sequential flow of control and this is messy. It makes following what is intended to happen difficult and it makes error handling very difficult.

The Promise

This is where the `Promise` object enters the picture. It is used to solve the problem of sequencing asynchronous operations. A `Promise` is an object that is provided by a function that would otherwise need a callback.

`Promise` has a `then` method which the consumer of the `Promise` uses to set callback functions which are executed on success or failure. For example:

```
myPromise.then(success,fail);
```

where *success* is the function called when the task finishes and the `Promise` resolves successfully and *fail* is called if it fails for any reason. You don't have to supply a fail function if you don't want to handle the error. The success function is passed a single value which can be used for the result of the operation - it is the "promised value". If a value isn't passed to the success function then the default is `undefined`.

For example, if we have a function called `delay(t)` which immediately returns a `Promise` which waits for t milliseconds to resolve and returns t as its value, we can use it to delay any other function:

```
delay(5000).then(function(t){alert("Delay Over after"+t+"ms");});
```

After five seconds you will see the alert message appear when the `Promise` resolves.

It is important to be very clear that the `delay` function returns immediately and the program carries on. The returned `Promise` object persists and the function supplied to the `then` method is called after the current code has completed.

Notice that the functions supplied to the `then` method, or other methods of the `Promise`, will not be called until the code has completed, even if the `Promise` is immediately resolved, or is resolved when the `then` method is called. For example, you can use:

```
Promise.resolve(value)
```

to return a resolved `Promise` that wraps the specified value.

Why would you want to do this? One reason is to run a function asynchronously:

```
console.log(41);
Promise.resolve(42).then(function(value){console.log(value)});
console.log(43);
```

This prints 41, 43 and 42 on the console. The reason is, of course that the function passed to `then` is only called after the current code has been run to completion.

The advantage of a `Promise` is that it implements a fluent interface and the `then` method returns a `Promise` so you can write:

```
let myPromise=delay(5000);
myPromise.then(function1).then(function2);
```

and `function2` will be called after `function1`. In other words, the function calls have been sequenced without callback hell. There are other advantages when it comes to error handling, but this is the most important idea.

For example, if we convert the earlier `getImage` function to return a `Promise`:

```
function getImage(imageURL){
 var img = new Image();
 img.src = imageURL;
 return new Promise(function(resolve,reject){
                  img.addEventListener('load', resolve, false);
                }
}
```

the `Promise` that `getImage` returns now only calls its `then` method when the image has loaded. So to call `function1` after the image has loaded you would use:

```
getImage(url1).then(function1);
```

As `then` returns a `Promise` you can now write a sequential image load as:

```
getImage(url1).then(function1).then(load second image);
```

There are also methods that let you run a function when one of a set of Promises resolves or after they all have. There is also a catch method, which is called if any of the Promises in a chain fails and this mimics the usual error handling in sequential code.

Promises do help with callback hell, but they are also about controlling the sequence of asynchronous operations. However, modern JavaScript has an even better way of doing this.

Async and Await

If you use the keyword async in front of a function then it is modified to return a Promise that resolves to the original return value of the function. You can think of async as automatically promise-ifying a function.

This is useful, but the clever part is the await operator, which can only be used within a function that has been declared with async. The await operator can be applied to any Promise. It has the effect of pausing the function and waiting for the Promise to resolve. That is, within an async function:

```
await myPromise;
```

stops the execution of the function at this instruction and the thread of execution returns to the code that called the function. When the Promise resolves the await either converts it to its returned value or, if the Promise is rejected, it throws an exception. You can see that the effect of the await is to hide the fact that a Promise is in use and to pause and resume the execution of the function. For example, the getImage can be used within an async function:

```
async function myFunction(){
  let result1=await getImage(url1);
  let result2=await getImage(url2);
}
```

In this case result1 and result2 are set to undefined as getImage doesn't return a value. Notice that there is no need to use a callback or a then as the await pauses the execution and allows the thread of execution to continue to process the code that called the function. The Promise cannot resolve until that code finishes running and the thread can process the event queue.

To make Promises and async/await work better, an additional event queue has been created - the microtask queue. Events are stored in the task queue and what happens is the queue is processed one task at a time in the order that they were added to the queue. What is new is that now when a task is completed the system checks the microtask queue and processes all of the microtasks until it is empty and only then does it move on to the next task.

You can see that microtasks have a higher priority than tasks. `Promises` are processed on the microtask queue and therefore a `Promise` will resolve before other events are processed.

There are other complications with the `async/await` approach to asynchronous code, but for simple applications it is cleaner and easier to understand. It is not so much `async/await` that is the jem, it is the way in which `async/await` meshes with `Promises` and callbacks to provide an elegant and flexible solution to writing asynchronous code. But it is the adoption of the "run-to-completion" principle that makes JavaScript really easy to async.

Jem 15

The Revealing Constructor Pattern

"Those that are most slow in making a promise are the most faithful in the performance of it."

Jean-Jacques Rousseau

There is no doubt that the `Promise` is a JavaScript jem. Other languages have Promises or something similar, but the JavaScript way of doing the job is amazing. We have just looked at the `Promise` along with `async/await`, but there is something more to learn by understand how Promises are implemented. There is something mysterious inside a `Promise` object that could well have other applications if it was better known.

You may think that you have Promises mastered, but do you really know how they work? The whole security of the `Promise` is based on the revealing constructor pattern, which is useful and a jem in its own right.

The idea of a Promise object is a clever one, but to implement it properly requires even more cleverness. Early attempts at creating a Promise were flawed and it took time to work out how to do it properly. The fact that is can be done properly without having to change JavaScript is an affirmation that JavaScript as a whole is a jem, but only if you understand it well enough.

Creating Promises

When you create a standard `Promise` you use its constructor and you pass it a single function, the *executor*, that is immediately executed by the constructor, for example:

```
let p=new Promise(executor);
```

The *executor* is the function where you create the asynchronous task and then call the Promise's `resolve` or `reject` methods accordingly – usually when the asynchronous task has completed. In other words, this is the code that does the work that you are interested in.

For example, the `delay` function introduced in Jem 14 can be written using JavaScript Promises as:

```
function delay(t) {
  var p = new Promise(
            function (resolve, reject) {
              setTimeout(
                function () {
                    resolve();
                },
              t);
            });
  return p;
}
```

You can see that this follows the pattern, creating a `Promise` by passing its constructor an executor function with `resolve` and `reject` as parameters. The executor function does what it has to do to complete the function's task and arranges to call ether `resolve` or `reject` according to whether or not the task is successfully completed. The constructor executes the executor immediately and it is important that the executor returns as quickly as possible. In the example, the executor sets up an asynchronous action, i.e. it calls `setTimeout`, and then returns. It is only much later, after t milliseconds, that the function specified in the `setTimeout` is executed and this calls `resolve` or `reject`. Notice that you supplied the executor function but `resolve` and `reject` are functions that are defined within the `Promise`

It is important that the functions `resolve` and `reject` are private to the `Promise` and only it and the executor have access to them. When we first began implementing `Promises` keeping them private was a problem. It was essential to provide functions so that the code that was using the `Promise` to signal when it was finished could change the state of the `Promise`, but the code that was consuming the `Promise`, using `then` and `catch` functions, was unable to change the state of the `Promise`.

That is, only the code that created the Promise should be able to set its state.

The earliest solution to this problem of keeping the internal state private was to use a two-object solution. This is the solution that jQuery adopted in the very early days of Promises and it is a lesson in why it is not always good to be a first adopter. jQuery uses two similar objects, the `Deferred` and the `Promise` to implement a standard Promise.

A `Deferred` object was used by the `Promise` creator to manage the Promise. The `Deferred` had the necessary functions to resolve and reject the Promise, and the `Promise` had all of the functions the consumer needed, like `then`. In practice, it was better to have the `Deferred` object also having all of the functions that `Promise` had and so `Deferred` looked like a "super-Promise" object. The `Deferred` object was kept private to the object that created the `Promise`, and was used by it to call `resolve` and `reject` methods that place the `Promise` in the resolved or reject state.

In retrospect this was probably a mistake as it results in a confusion between what the Deferred is, and what it is used for. If you wanted to, you could pass the `Deferred` object to the user rather than the `Promise` object and this would allow them to change the internal state.

The two-object solution to keeping the `resolve` and `reject` functions private was solved by the generalization of the mechanism long used to keep methods and properties private to an object. That is, in place of a private `Deferred` object which has the `accept` and `reject` methods, in the Promise's standard both `resolve` and `reject` are private methods of the `Promise` object itself.

This all works but there is a better way.

Private Methods

Modern Promises use a modification on the standard way that constructors provide private methods called the revealing constructor pattern. You don't need to understand how this works to consume or even produce Promises, but it isn't difficult and it might well have other uses so it is worth knowing about. Like all JavaScript patterns, once you have seen it, it seems more than obvious.

First let's see how to create a private method – if you are sure you know how, skip to the next section.

A private method is one that is created as a closure when an object is created. This is the standard method for creating a private variable accessible from within an object, but not from outside. The only difference is that the variable references a function.

For example, to create a private variable:

```
function myConstructor(){
  var private=0;
  this.myFunction=function(){
              alert(private);
          }
}
```

This is a constructor for an object with just one method, `myFunction`.

The important part is the variable `private`. This is not part of the object because it isn't declared as a property of the object. so if you try:

```
var myObject=new myConstructor();
myObject.private=1;
```

you will see an error that `private` doesn't exist. However, as `private` is in scope when `myFunction` is declared, it is available to it as a closure. That is:

```
myObject.myFunction();
```

does display the value of `private`.

A private method uses the same mechanism with the small difference that the variable references a function – an inner function which is not a method of the object being constructed.

This is the mechanism that the JavaScript `Promise` uses to make `resolve` and `reject` private methods, but with some additional twists. The main twist is that private functions and variables are accessed by a function that is passed to the constructor i.e. the executor.

Let's see how this works. Suppose you need to set a private variable to some value when the constructor is used but after that it is private and inaccessible. The simplest solution is:

```
function myClass(value){
  var myPrivateVar=value;
  this.myMethod=function(){
                  console.log(myPrivateVar);
                }
}
```

Now you can create an instance using:

```
var myObject=new myClass(10);
myObject.myMethod();
```

The value of the private variable will be printed, i.e. `10`, and this has been set when the constructor was used, but the variable cannot now be altered by code external to the object.

This seems simple enough, but if we push the idea just a little further it gets a little bit more difficult. What happens if you want to pass a function in the constructor call that works with private members of the object being constructed? The function is intended to be executed by the constructor as the object is being created. A first attempt might be something like:

```
function myClass(func) {
 var myPrivateVar = Math.random();
 var reveal = function (){
                     return myPrivateVar;
                   }
 func();
}
```

This creates a private variable set to a random value which can be discovered by accessing the private method `reveal` and `func` is a function, passed into the constructor and then executed, which can make use of `reveal` to access the value. The idea is that we are trying to allow the passed in function access to private variables that the object being constructed has access to only because of closure.

If you try it out by passing it a function that tries to make use of `reveal`:

```
var myObject = new myClass(
        function () { console.log(reveal()); }
            );
```

you will see an error message generated when `func` is called saying the reveal is undefined.

The error here is obvious, `reveal` is not in scope for the function passed into the constructor. Which variables a function can access is determined by where the function is declared, not where it is used. That is, the variables `myPrivateVar` and `reveal` are not global to the function passed in. They exist, but they are out of scope.

It might be easier to see this if we re-write the use of the constructor to show more clearly where the function is defined:

```
let myFunc=function () { console.log(reveal()); }
var myObject = new myClass(myFunc);
```

The Revealing Constructor

The solution to the mistake is simple enough – pass the required private members as parameters to the function. This is what you do whenever you need a function to work with values that exist but are not in scope - that's what parameters are for. For example:

```
var myObject = new myClass(
        function (reveal) { console.log(reveal()); }
        );
```

Note that the function needs to be called within the constructor with a parameter:

```
function myClass(func) {
  var myPrivateVar = Math.random();
  var reveal = function () { return myPrivateVar;};
  func(reveal);
}
```

Now it all works but it looks very strange.

When you look at the constructor call you get the uneasy feeling that it is wrong because `reveal` hasn't been defined - it isn't in scope. However, `reveal` in this case is a parameter in the function definition and nothing to do with any `reveal` that is within the constructor.

The function passed to the constructor can call private functions within the constructor as long as they are passed to it when the function is called.

Notice that you can just as well write:

```
var myObject = new myClass(
            function (firstParameter) {
                console.log(firstParameter());}
            );
```

The name used for the first parameter is irrelevant just like that of any parameter – it only has meaning within the function that it is a parameter of. The value of the first parameter, i.e. the function to be passed in, only becomes fixed when the constructor calls the function. That is, when it reaches:

```
func(reveal);
```

Notice that, after the constructor has finished its job, no other function can call `reveal` except for methods of the object constructed. It is private to the object and only accessible by closure.

The general principles of the revealing constructor pattern are:

- Local variables, and hence inner functions within an object's constructor, are private to the constructor and the object it constructs.
- The object gains access to these private variables by closure.
- Private members can be accessed by the code that calls the constructor by passing parameters.
- If the code that calls the constructor passes a function that is executed by the constructor, it cannot access the private variables because they were not in scope when the function was defined.
- Private variables can be passed to the function as they are in scope when the constructor calls the function.

The revealing constructor pattern is generally useful to allow external code restricted access to private functions within a constructor. It is, of course, how the Promise constructor allows you access to the resolve and reject functions - but only within the constructor – and this makes it a jem.

Functional And Not Quite Functional

"Whoever said that pleasure wasn't functional?"

Charles Eames

Functional programming is a programming paradigm that has a gained a great deal of popularity recently and JavaScript can be used in a functional style. This isn't surprising as it was inspired by the functional language, Scheme. However there are "degrees" of functional programming depending on how strict you want to be in applying its basic principles.

Most programmers who adopt a functional style don't go the whole way and essentially make use of the easy and rewarding parts of the idea. This isn't necessarily a bad thing, but it does leave you open to criticism that you don't really know what functional is - so let's put that right.

The Essence of Functional Programming

Functional languages try to reduce, or is it enhance, programming languages to mathematical functions. That is, when you use a mathematical function its result never changes - the result of `sin(0.3)` is always the same - and a function is just a lookup table. Sometimes the lookup table is too big to be stored and in this case the result is returned after being calculated using a procedure - but in theory all mathematical functions can be implemented as lookup tables. Converting a function that produces a result by calculation into one that stores the results in a lookup table is often referred to as memoization.

That is, mathematical functions provide a way to do computation without any dynamic change. A function returns its result and it is the same result for the same input. It is static and stateless.

This isn't so with the procedural programming meaning of functions or procedures. In the programming context, a function is just a procedure that returns a single value as its result. All procedures can be cast as functions by the simple trick of having them return a single, but perhaps complicated structure, containing all their results rolled up into one object. That is, in general, a function can accept and return objects including other functions.

This is usually expressed as functional programming needs "first class functions". Of course, in JavaScript functions are just objects that can be invoked using the invocation operator () - so they are first class by default. It is also common to call a function that accepts or returns another function a "higher order function".

A programming function can produce "side effects" and state changes, for example:

```
function addone(){
 globalvariable=globalvariable+1;
  return globalvariable
}
```

In this case each time the function is called it returns a new value - it is counting - it is procedural - and this can't be allowed in a functional language. In addition, it changes a global variable and this is a side effect. If another function makes use of the same global then its behavior will have been changed.

A function that gives the same result every time it is called with the same parameters and one that has no side effects is called a pure function. The goal of functional programming is to use nothing but pure functions.

In a functional language the sort of counting described above isn't allowed and variables aren't variable in the sense that once defined they have that value for the duration of the program - they are "bound" to their value. In other words, all objects are immutable. Once created an object cannot be changed.

At this point non-functional programmers generally give up because this is nothing like the way they think. How can there be loops and conditions if variables never change? How can the counting function be implemented in a pure way with immutable objects?

There are two answers to this question. The first is why are you counting at all? If the counting is part of an algorithm that gets you to a solution then don't do it - simply get the solution. That is, if you implement sin(0.3) with an iterative calculation, simply hide the iteration behind the function and return the result. In other words pretend that there is no iteration involved and leave it to hidden non-functional implementations.

The second answer is that there are functional ways of doing the same job, mostly recursion and functional composition. For example, if f(x) is a function which returns x+1 then counting can be implemented as:

```
x=0;
y=f(x);
z=f(f(x));
```

and so on...

Notice that in the set of nested functions:

```
z=f(f(f(f(f(f(f(x)))))));
```

only one variable z is bound to the result, no variables change their values and yet even so there is still an "increment" as you work your way into the brackets.

This is how pure functions can be used to count. In principle the function does something with the count, much as you would in a for loop say. This is, the functional language's equivalent of the fixed repeat for loop. There are also equivalents of for loops that perform variable numbers of repeat using either functional composition or recursion.

For example, if you want to count down from N to 0 you would use:

```
function count(N){
    if(N===0)return;
    count(N-1);
}
```

Notice that as N is used as a parameter its value isn't changed as a new N comes into existence each time the function is called. Some programmers take to recursion and some don't. Recursion is natural for some problems and less so for others. Notice that this is a pure function, but if you put an ??alert in the body to display the count it has a side effect and is no longer pure.

So the main principles of functional programming are:

- First class functions – for function composition and higher order functions.
- Pure functions - functions always return the same output for the same input and have no side effects.
- Immutable data - data is never changed once created and new data is created in place of mutation.
- Recursion is a natural way of avoiding mutating data and provides an alternative to iteration.

How strictly these are obeyed varies a great deal and you can program in a way that is slightly functional, mostly functional or hard line, that is nothing but functional styles. In many cases programmers opt to take the immediate advantages of functional programming by using first class functions, functional composition and higher order functions, but tend to be less concerned about avoiding side effects, allowing mutable data and using recursion.

Functional Programming in JavaScript

There are libraries that make it easier to program in a functional style in JavaScript, but the language already has enough facilities for a reasonable approach to functional programming.

The most obvious functional programming aspect of JavaScript is that it has first class functions which makes functional composition and higher order functions trivial. This is not the place to go over these ideas as they have been covered in other jems, but there are plenty of examples in what follows. Perhaps the biggest problems with functional JavaScript is that side effects are the norm, unless you go to extreme lengths, and mutability is the default.

JavaScript may not be a functional programming language but it does have first class functions and this makes it very easy to create and use higher order functions.

It is also important to point out that the lambda or arrow functions introduced in Jem 11 have very little to do with functional programming. That is JavaScript isn't more functional because it now has lambda functions. It is true that the lambda calculus influenced functional programming and lambda functions as found in many languages refer to this, but they are simply syntactic sugar and anything you can do with an arrow function you can do with a standard function. They are useful but they aren't "deep".

JavaScript isn't a functional language but it does have some features which lend themselves to a sort of functional programming - perhaps function-oriented programming, FOP, is a better name and we'll return to it in Jem18. Immutable data and iterators are discussed in other jems, here we will look at higher order functions.

Higher Order Functions

As already stated, more than once, JavaScript has first class functions and this is a jem. As they are first class functions they can be higher order functions, which simply means they accept functions as parameters or return functions as a result. If you have programmed in JavaScript at all you will almost certainly have encountered higher order functions in the context of callbacks. Any function that asks you to supply a callback function to use when it has finished is by definition a higher order function. However, as explained in Jem 14, higher order functions are for more than just callbacks. Higher order functions are everywhere in JavaScript, but we tend not to think of using the same ideas with our own functions.

For example, if you wanted to time how long a function takes to execute you could write a decorator to modify any function:

```
function timeFunction(f) {
    return function (...args) {
        var t1 = performance.now();
        var result = f(...args);
        t1 = performance.now() - t1;
        console.log(t1);
        return result;
    };
}
```

The `performance.now` method gives millisecond accurate timing, but you can use the `now` method as an alternative. The important general points are that the arguments are passed using the rest parameters operator, which creates `args` as an array out of however many parameters are passed, and the destructuring operator is used to pass as many parameters as were supplied. Confusingly both these operators are ... that is three dots. Notice that this allows the creation of a higher function that can accept a function that takes any number of parameters and call it without having to know the number of parameters in advance.

For example, you can create a function with three parameters:

```
function sum(a, b, c) {
    return a + b + c;
}
```

and pass it to another function `timeFunction` to add the timing instructions:

```
sum= timeFunction(sum);
console.log(sum(1, 2, 3));
```

Notice that the change to the function is permanent. If you want a temporary change then assign the modified function to a new variable.

Perhaps the best known and most used higher order functions are `map`, `filter` and `reduce`. These accept a function as a parameter and apply the function to every element of a collection. So impressive are these higher order functions in making code more compact, and more importantly understandable, that they are often the reason for an initial interest in functional programming. They are perhaps the main reason some programmers adopt FOP without going the whole way to functional programming. More of these higher order functions in Jem 18: Functional Approach to Iteration.

Partial Application and Currying

Two important examples of higher functions that you are almost certain to meet if you continue to explore functional programming are partial application and the mysterious sounding currying. They are related ways of deriving new functions from old.

The first, partial application is very easy to understand. If you have a function of n parameters then partial application is simply deriving a new function based on fixing a subset of the parameters to particular values.

For example, the three-parameter sum given in the last section:

```
function sum(a, b, c) {
        return a + b + c;
    }
```

can be reduced to a two-parameter sum by supplying the first parameter:

```
sum(1, b, c);
```

You can easily write a higher order function that will reduce a general function to use one fewer parameters:

```
 function partialApp(f, p1) {
    return function (...args) {
            return f(p1, ...args);
        };
 }
```

The three-parameter sum function can be reduced to a two-parameter sum function using:

```
const sum2 = partialApp(sum, 1);
console.log(sum2(2, 3));
```

Notice that now the sum2 function computes the sum of b plus c incremented by 1. In general a partially applied function computes a sub-function of the original. You can easily generalize partialApp so that it partially applies the first m parameters. Alternatively you can use the bind method:

```
const sum2=sum.bind(null,1);
```

which sets the function's this parameter, see Jem 4, to null and the first parameter to 1 and returns the partially applied function. If you supply more parameters they are all partially applied in order. For example:

```
const sum1=sum.bind(null,1,2);
```

sets a to 1 and b to 2 leaving only c to be specified.

What is more difficult is to write a function that partially applies an arbitrary set of parameters i.e. in any order.

This brings us to currying, named in honor of logician Haskell Curry (the functional language Haskell is also a tribute to him). Currying is like partial application but it reduces a multi-parameter function to a series of single-parameter higher order functions each one returning a function of the next parameter.

The best way to understand how this works is to manually curry our three-parameter sum function:

```
function currySum(a){
        return function(b){
                return function(c){
                        return a+b+c;
                };
        };
};
```

When you call currySum(1) it returns a function that accepts the b parameter and returns a function that accepts the c parameter and finally works out the result. Notice that the final function has access to a and b because of closure. In general, only languages that support closure make currying easy.

It is usual to call a curried function using repeated invocation:

```
const ans=currySum(1)(2)(3);
```

At first this might look a little strange and it hides the fact that we really do have increasingly specialized functions. For example, in:

```
const S1=currySum(1);
```

S1 is a function that adds 1 to its parameter and in:

```
const S2=S1(2);
```

S2 is a function that adds 1 and 2 to its parameter and finally:

```
const ans=S2(3);
```

adds 1 and 2 to 3 to give 6.

You can see that currying is different from partial application as you get a set of one-parameter functions that do the same job rather than just a general reduction in the number of parameters.

However, consider:

```
const S1=currySum(1);
```

This is a single-parameter function, but you can call it using functional composition:

```
const ans=S1(b)(c);
```

You can see that S1 is behaving a bit like a two-parameter function and you can turn it into a two-parameter function quite easily:

```
function S12(b,c){
      return S1(b)(c)
};
```

This is the connection between currying and partial application.

So what are they for? A good question. If you are keen on functional programming then they are their own reward. If not you probably have to keep a close eye on what you are doing to spot an opportunity where currying or partial application pays dividends. Typically this sort of parameter reduction is useful when you have a situation where a particular variation on a function is going to be used repeatedly. For example, suppose we have a bonus of the day function which varies according to the day:

```
function bonusDay(day,amount){....}
```

then on Monday you might curry or partial the function to:

```
const bonus=partialApp(bonusDay,"mon");
```

and use the:

```
bonus(amount);
```

function in the rest of the program instead of having to supply the day of the week each time.

Basically whenever you are going to call a function with the same argument over and over consider partial evaluation or currying.

Functional Composition and Fluent Style

At its simplest, functional composition just means calling a function to operate on the result of an earlier function.

If you have function F and function G then you can compose them as:

```
F(G(p));
```

Simple, but notice that this only works if G returns an object which F is expecting to work with. If F is expecting a number and G returns a non-numeric object then clearly the composition will not work. Also notice that although the composition is written F followed by G it is G that is evaluated first and then F.

The way that the output of one function becomes the input to another lets us think in terms of function "pipelines" and this in turn suggests fluent interfaces or chaining. Currying takes us one step towards a fluent interface. If function F returns function G then we can write:

```
F()(p)
```

and things are happening in the order written.

Take this one stage further, and have function F return an object with function G as a method and we can write:

```
F.G(p)
```

and so on,.. and fluent style is born.

For a bigger example, consider the DSL for arithmetic introduced in Jem 7. The functions involved - sqrt, square, times and display - could be implemented as functions that return a numeric value and a calculation could be written as:

```
display(times(3,display(square(display(sqrt(100))))));
```

As you can see, the problem is that the nested brackets make it difficult to get right.

If instead of functional composition we allow each function to return an object which has the necessary functions as methods, then this can be written as:

```
var c = new CalcConstruct();
    c.setValue(100)
      .sqrt()
      .display()
      .square()
      .display()
      .times(3)
      .display();
```

See Jem 12: Fluent Interfaces for more detail.

Arguably fluent interfaces or chaining make functional composition easier to work with. In particular, notice that the order in which the functions are carried out is the same as they are written.

Fluent style is one of the things that attracts beginners to the use of functions, even if it isn't the full functional approach.

So JavaScript's first class functions are a jem, but we already know this. What makes them even better is that the way that the arguments object, rest, spread and bind all make it possible to really work with functions in higher order functions. The way that it fits together is indeed a jem.

Jem 17

Immutability

> *"God made thee perfect, not immutable."*
>
> *John Milton*

Immutable variables and objects are very much part of strict functional programming, but immutability also has uses in more general settings. Defining an immutable object is simple - its an object whose state cannot change. They are also safe to share between different processes for exactly the same reason. In JavaScript you cannot share objects between processes in this way and so some of the attraction of immutable objects is lost.

If you are going to pursue strict functional programming then you are probably better off with a different language - one that enforces immutability and gives you the tools to work with it. JavaScript gives you just enough to do some of the job, but it is the part of the job you most often want to do and you gain the most benefit from. So even its partial approach to immutability is a jem.

In JavaScript immutability is more about making an object secure from accidental or even malicious modifications. There seems to be little point in implementing custom immutable data structures as, without the involvement of the runtime, the implementation is going to be inefficient. It may be that immutable is safe, but mutable is powerful and it is what makes programming different from mathematics. In many cases a bit of mutation saves the day, and so it to can also be considered a jem.

Immutable Variables

You can implement immutable objects and "variables" in JavaScript. If you declare a variable to be `const` then it is immutable. However, what it references can still be mutable. For example, you can declare a `const` variable and make it reference an object:

```
const myObj={};
```

You can then change properties of the object:

```
myObj.newProperty=42;
```

However, if you try to assign a different object to the variable:

```
myObj={};
```

a runtime error occurs. The variable is immutable, but what it references isn't.

If you are attempting to use JavaScript in a functional style then all of your variable declarations should in principle be `const`. There is a good argument that even if you don't follow functional style, all variables should be `const` until it is proved they need to be declared `let` or `var`.

Immutable Strings And Mutable Arrays

Before looking at immutability more generally, it is worth examining the JavaScript `Array` and `String` - these are good examples of mutable versus immutable data structures. The `Array` is mutable and the `String` is immutable and makes a good archetype for understanding immutable objects.

The key difference between these two basic data structures is that you can modify an element of an `Array`, but you cannot modify the "elements" of a `String`. For example, to change the fourth element of an `Array` you would use:

```
const myArray=[1,2,3,4,5];
myArray[3]=0;
alert(myArray);
```

which results in `1,2,3,0,5` being displayed.

Compare this to changing the fourth character of a `String`:

```
const myString="12345";
const newString=myString.substr(0,3)+"0"+myString.substr(4);
alert(newString);
```

In this case there is no way to directly modify the fourth element. Instead you have to tear the string apart and put it back together with the new character in place of the old. The result is a new string and the old string is unmodified. All string methods and operations are like this. They work on the original string and produce a new string. This is the sense in which strings are immutable and yet we hardly notice this as we are so familiar with this way of working with them.

When thinking about immutability in more general contexts it often helps to think about the contrast between the way you work with arrays and strings.

Levels Of Immutability

If you want to make an object immutable you have a choice of three methods, `seal`, `preventExtensions` and `freeze`. These provide three different levels of immutability.

The `seal` method stops you from adding, removing or reconfiguring properties. However, you can change what they reference. Basically a sealed object can be used as if it was mutable, but you cannot change the "structure" or "type" of the object.

The `preventExtensions` method works in the same way as `seal`, but you can remove properties.

The `freeze` method is like `seal`, but it also makes the properties immutable. You can't assign new values to the properties in addition to not being able to change them in other ways. Thus, `freeze` is about as close as you can get to a true immutable object, but notice that while it makes properties immutable it doesn't make the objects that the properties reference immutable. That is, `freeze` is shallow and doesn't freeze sub-objects of an object. If you want a "deep freeze" you have to explicitly `freeze` each object referenced by the first object and so on until you reach a primitive value.

In all three cases you can change properties of the prototype object unless it has been made immutable and all three operations are irreversible. The only way to get a mutable object from an immutable object is to clone it.

One problem is that the standard doesn't specify precisely what should happen if you try to modify a sealed or frozen object - it might just fail silently or it might cause a runtime error. For example, if we create an object with a property and then `seal` it, we cannot add another property:

```
const myObj = {};
myObj.newProperty1 = 42;
Object.seal(myObj);
myObj.newProperty1 = 43;
myObj.newProperty2 = 43;
alert(myObj.newProperty1);
alert(myObj.newProperty2);
```

Exactly what you see depends on how the error is handled. In Chrome the creation of the new property fails silently and you see 43 in the first alert box and undefined in the second.

If you change `seal` to `freeze`:

```
Object.freeze(myObj);
```

then you will see 42 in the first alert box, as you now cannot change a property's reference, and `undefined` in the second, as you still cannot modify the object by adding a property.

Notice that there is no way to undo any of these three methods. Your only option if you want to make changes to an immutable object is to make a clone. Making a deep clone in JavaScript isn't easy. You can make a shallow clone very easily in a number of different ways. The most direct is to use the `assign` method:

```
Object.assign(target,sources)
```

where *target* is the object that the properties in *sources*, a comma separated list of objects, are added to. You can use `assign` to merge objects or create a shallow copy of an object, even if it is immutable. For example:

```
const myObj2=Object.assign({},myObj);
```

copies all of the properties of `myObj` and adds them to the empty object to create a shallow copy of `myObj`. That is, `myObj2` has all of the own and enumerable properties of `myObj` and these are set to the same values as the properties of `myObj`. If `myObj` has a property that references another object then `myObj2` has a property of the same name that references the same, and not a copy of, that object. Also if `myObj` has getters and setters then `myObj2` has properties that have the values that the getters and setters return, not the getter and setter functions. Finally, properties on the prototype chain are not copied.

If the reference to the immutable object is mutable then you can replace it by a mutable clone. If the reference is immutable, i.e. `const`, you cannot do this.

Put simply, making a mutable object immutable is easy, but reversing the action is hard.

If you need a general solution then the best advice is to use a library such as lodash, which provides a tested and maintained deep clone function.

Working With Immutable Objects

So how do you actually work with immutable objects?

The simple answer is that you have to add methods that avoid mutation by making a copy complete with the modification. As we have just noted, making an accurate copy of a general object is difficult, but for specific objects with known characteristics it is easier.

For example, consider an object suitable to record a name and phone number:

```
person = {name: "mickey",
          phone: "424242"
        };
```

The usual, mutating, way of recording a name change is:

```
person.name = "minnie";
```

If you freeze the object this will not work and you need to provide a method that will create a new object with the new value. There are many ways of doing this, but using `assign` is particularly simple:

```
person = {name: "mickey",
          phone: "424242",
          setName:function (newname) {
                   return Object.assign({},this, {name:newname} );
                }
        };
```

Notice that we use three objects in the call to `assign`. The first is the new object that all of the properties in `this` are copied to and the third a temporary object with a new value for the name property which overwrites the name property merged from `this`.

Using the immutable version is slightly more complicated:

```
const updatedPerson = person.setName("minnie");
```

Here you need a modifier function for each property and even one that sets multiple properties by passing an object. For example:

```
set: function (newValues) {
                   return Object.assign({}, this, newValues);
        }
```

To set both properties you could use:

```
const updatedPerson = person.set({name:"minnie",phone:"123456"});
```

Notice that the new `updatedPerson` object has a `setName` or `set` function, but it is the same function defined in `person`. That is, if you change the function in `person` it is changed in `updatedPerson` and you can think of `person` as being a sort of prototype for objects cloned from it. Usually this is the behavior you want.

One complication is that if you want to do the job properly and create a prototype object with all of the functions to share among all of the instances of the person object then you also have to explicitly `set` the prototype of the clone, as `assign` doesn't clone the prototype. For example:

```
const personPrototype = {
        set: function (newValues) {
                return Object.assign(Object.create(personPrototype),
                                                   this, newValues);
                }
        };

const person = Object.create(personPrototype)
person.name = "mickey";
person.phone = "424242"


Object.freeze(person);
person.name = "minnie";
const updatedPerson = person.set({name: "minnie", phone: "123456"});
alert(person.name);
alert(updatedPerson.name);
```

In this case we have followed the general principle of putting all of the methods in the prototype object - which is just the `set` method in this example. The `set` method creates a null object with the correct prototype and the original object is cloned and modified.

The ability to create immutable objects is a jem as it is so easy to use, but the fact that you cannot create a deep clone is something of a problem.

Jem 18

Functional Approach To Iteration

"Few ideas work on the first try. Iteration is key to innovation."

Sebastian Thrun

The functional approach to iteration is probably the main reason that programmers are initially attracted to the idea of functional programming. Using it is a compact and direct way to express the idea of doing something with a collection of data entities and it leads on naturally to fluent interfaces, which share many of the same characteristics. It also generalizes to the idea of using functions, even if they are impure and don't conform well to the broader tenets of functional programming simply because they express the intent of the program better than the equivalent control structures. This utilitarian approach to using functions isn't quite functional programming and you might as well call it function-oriented programming or FOP.

Let's see how all this arises from the familiar `Array` object.

Arrays and For Loops

Arrays are the simplest of data structures and they pair perfectly with the for loop, providing us with the first example of a data structure determining the program structure used to process it. If you have an `Array A` then each element is indexed by an integer and to process the elements of the `Array` all you have to do is iterate the index using a `for` loop:

```
const myArray=["a","b","c"];
for(let i=0;i<3;i++){
   console.log(myArray[i].toUpperCase());
}
```

You can see that the idea is that we repeat the operation on the `Array` for i set to 0, 1 and 2 - we "step through" the array processing it as we go.

In many cases the index i and the element `myArray[i]` are both needed, but sometimes you just need the element `myArray[i]`. In such cases you can use the `for of` loop. which steps through an array in the same order as the index:

```
const myArray=["a","b","c"];
for(const element of myArray){
    console.log(element.toUpperCase());
 }
```

In the case where you only want the index, you can use a `for in` loop:

```
const myArray=["a","b","c"];
for(const index in myArray){
    console.log(index));
 }
```

We'll look at why you might want to do this later.

Functional For

For loops and arrays go together, but there is a way of packaging `for` that makes it disappear. `Array` has a `forEach` method that will apply a function that you supply to each element in an array. The function is supplied with three arguments - the current element, the index and the entire array. All of the parameters are optional and usually only `element` and perhaps `index` are used. For example:

```
const myArray = ["a", "b", "c"];
myArray.forEach(function (element)
                {
                  console.log(element.toUpperCase());
                }
                );
```

does the same job as the `for` loop and the `for of` loop in the previous section. It looks easier to understand and if you write it using an arrow function it is even more compact:

```
myArray.forEach( element => console.log(element.toUpperCase()) );
```

Many beginners are impressed by `forEach`, or one of the many similar functions, and they tend not to ask "where did the for loop go?" The answer, however, is fairly obvious and you can see that the `forEach` method is just equivalent to:

```
function forEach(f){
  for(const index in myArray){
      f(this[index],index,this);
  }
}
```

So it isn't mysterious or even clever, but it is attractive to use.

There are `Array` methods that hide for loops and the best known is `map` which works like `forEach`, but creates a new array using the return value of the function. For example:

```
const myArray = ["a", "b", "c"];
const myArray2 = myArray.map(function (element) {
                            return element.toUpperCase();
                            }
                          );
console.log(myArray2);
```

Notice that in this case the `map` method returns a new Array with the result, in the spirit of immutability. The function that is applied to each element has to return the new value of each element. Don't use `map` if you don't modify the array as it is just a waste of memory to create a new array you don't want.

The second most well known function of this kind is probably `reduce`. This doesn't just take each element in turn and modify it, it also keeps a running sum. The `reduce` method really does reduce an array to a single result. The function that you pass to it has four parameters – the accumulator for the running sum, the current element, the index and the entire array. You also have to optionally pass an initial value for the accumulator and although optional, in practice it is usually essential. For example, to sum the elements of an `Array` you would use:

```
const myArray = [1, 2, 3, 4, 5, 6];
const sum = myArray.reduce(function (acc, element) {
                            return element + acc;
                            }
                          ,0);
console.log(sum);
```

The initial value of the accumulator is set to zero and then each element is added to it in turn.

The call to `reduce` is equivalent to:

```
let acc=0;
for(const element of myArray){
    acc = element + acc;
}
```

Notice that `reduce` in its simplest form is different from the other array methods that "hide" a for loop because it really does reduce an array to a single value. However, it doesn't have to. The power of "everything is an object" means that `reduce` can be used in ways that don't reduce anything.

For example:

```
const myArray = [1, 2, 3, 4, 5, 6];
const mycopy = myArray.reduce(function (acc, element) {
                             acc.push(element);
                             return acc;
                     } ,[]);
console.log(mycopy);
```

Notice that the accumulator, acc, is initialized to a null array. This means that you can use it as an array in the update function and, for example, call its push method which adds the element to the end of the array. The result is a complete copy of the array rather than anything reduced.

You can see that it is possible to use reduce to do any of the jobs that map can do. Once you allow everything to be an object you do open up this sort of possibility.

A very common idiom is to chain this sort of method together in a fluent style. For example:

```
function square(x){ return x*x; }
function sum(x,y){ return x+y; }

const myArray = [1, 2, 3, 4, 5, 6];
console.log(myArray.map(square).reduce(sum));
```

computes the sum of squares of myArray. Notice, however, that this only works because map returns an Array that you can call reduce on and this involves two complete passes through the Array whereas an explicit for loop, or even forEach, would have done the job in one pass. This is inefficient and when you add it to the fact that map and reduce are generally slower than for loops, you can see that there is a cost to be paid for the clarity of expression.

One of the reasons for map/reduce to be a preferred way of writing advanced code is that they lend themselves to being computed on a parallel computer. The map can be split up between different processors each working on a different part of the array and the reduce can be computed in the same way, but with the different processors passing their results to a single collecting processor. This is the basis of parallel systems such as Hadoop, but there are no such advantages for JavaScript.

There are lots of similar array methods and you can look them up in the documentation, but here is a list and brief description accurate at the time of writing:

`every(test(element))`	tests every element in turn and returns true if they all test true
`filter(test(element))`	tests every element in turn and returns a new array with elements that test true
`find(test(element))`	returns the first element for which test is true
`findIndex(element))`	returns the index of the first element for which the test is true
`flat(depth)`	returns a new array with nested arrays flattened to the specified depth
`flatMap(function(element),depth)`	same as map(function(element)).flat(depth)
`forEach(function(element))`	apply the function to each element and only modify array if the function does.
`includes(value)`	true if value is an element
`indexOf(value)`	returns the first index of the value if in array or -1 otherwise
`join()`	concatenates each element as a string
`lastIndexOf(value)`	returns the last index of the value if in array or -1 otherwise
`map(function(element))`	returns a new array resulting from applying function to each element
`reduce(function(element,acc),init)`	apply function to each element setting acc to init and passing it to all calls to function
`reduceRight(function,initial)`	as for reduce but applied from right to left, i.e. high index values first
`reverse()`	reverse the values in the array in place - mutating
`slice(begin,end)`	return array from begin to end
`some(test)`	returns true if an element of the array makes test true
`sort()`	sorts array in place - mutating

There are also methods that involve partial scanning of the array, but these are the classic "hide the for loop" methods.

Map And Set

ES 2015 introduced two new data structures - `Map` and `Set` - which are also enumerable, that is they fit together with a `for` loop in the same way as `Array`. It is a shame that there is now a confusion between `Map`, the object and `map`, the function but both are reasonable choices.

The `Map` object is essentially a basic `Object` but with modifications to make it better suited for a role as a data structure. A `Map` object can be used to store key value pairs, just like an `Object`, but with differences:

- Map objects have properties like any object but they also have elements which are distinct from properties.
- Elements have to be added using the set method and retrieved using the get method.
- The key can be any value or object but for `Object` the `Key` has to be a `String` or a `Symbol`.
- There is a `size` property which gives you the number of elements.
- Iterating over a `Map` returns elements in the order they were inserted.
- A `Map` has no default elements.

Notice that a `Map` is still an object and you can add properties and hence methods, but these are not considered to be elements of the `Map`. For example:

```
const myMap=new Map();
myMap.set("mykey1","myvalue1");
myMap.set("mykey2","myvalue2");
myMap.myProperty=42;
console.log(myMap.size);
```

creates a `Map` with two elements and one property and hence `size` is 2.

You can use `for of` to iterate over the elements ignoring their properties:

```
for (element of myMap){
   console.log(element);
}
```

In this case elements are returned as two-element arrays `[key,value]` so the loop displays:

```
["mykey1", "myvalue1"]
["mykey2", "myvalue2"]
```

If you use `for in` instead what you iterate over are the `Map` object's enumerable properties:

```
for (element in myMap){
 console.log(element);
}
```

which displays:

```
myProperty
```

The different behavior is due to the difference between iterable and enumerable, which are discussed later.

Set is like Map in that it has iterable elements and enumerable properties, but each element is a single unique value. You add elements to the set using the add method and the size property gives you how many elements are stored. If you try to add an element that is already in the Set an additional element isn't added, but this is not an error. You can use for in and for of in the same way as for Map and you get the same sort of result:

```
const mySet=new Set();

mySet.add("myvalue1");
mySet.add("myvalue2");

mySet.myProperty=42;

for (element of mySet){
        console.log(element);
}

for (element in mySet){
        console.log(element);
}
```

The for of displays:

```
myvalue1
myvalue2
```

and the for in displays:

```
myProperty
```

At this point you might expect an explanation of how to use map, reduce, filter and so on with Map and Set, but the only function of this sort that they have is forEach:

```
forEach(function(value,key));
```

and for Set:

```
forEach(function(value));
```

which applies the function to each element and not to any properties, i.e. it is a functional wrapper around for of. You can, of course, add your own implementations of such functions using forEach, but standard implementations are not provided.

For example, to add map to Map:

```
const myMap = new Map();
myMap.map = function (f) {
            const acc = new Map();
            this.forEach(function (value,key) {
                    acc.set(key, f(value));
                }
            );
            return acc;
        };
```

```
myMap.set("mykey1", "myvalue1");
myMap.set("mykey2", "myvalue2");
myMap.myProperty = 42;
const myMap2=myMap.map(function (s) {return s.toUpperCase(); });
for (element of myMap2) { console.log(element); }
```

First we add a new method, map, to the instance of Map and then use it to apply a function to each of the elements of myMap. This is the simplest possible implementation with no error checking or handling, but it illustrates the fundamental idea.

If you want to add the map method to all Map instances simply allocate it to the prototype object:

```
Map.prototype.map = function (f) {
                const acc = new Map();
                this.forEach(function (value, key) {
                        acc.set(key, f(value));
                    }
                );
                return acc;
            };
const myMap = new Map();
```

Now you will find that myMap has a map method. Adding to the prototype of a built-in object in this way is generally discouraged, but it is JavaScript's equivalent of "extension" methods which are found in other languages and is regarded as perfectly respectable.

Enumerable Versus Iterable

In the discussion of Map and Set we encountered the difference between enumerable property and iterable elements. Most languages do not make this distinction, but JavaScript does in order to solve a problem introduced by "everything is an object". The problem occurs when you try to use an object as a data structure. Objects have properties and for data structures these properties can be internal properties, such as methods, or they can be elements of the data structure.

For example, if you create an object suitable for use as a name and telephone record or structure you might use something like:

```
const myPerson={name:"mickey",
               phone:"123456"
               };
for (key in myPerson){
        console.log(key);
        console.log(myPerson[key]);
}
```

and you will see displayed:

```
name
micky
phone
123456
```

which is exactly what you want.

However, if you add a method to the object:

```
const myPerson = {name: "mickey",
               phone: "123456",
               format: function () { this.name.toUpperCase(); }
               };
```

when you run the `for in` loop you see:

```
name
mickey
phone
123456
format
ƒ () {
     this.name.toUpperCase();
    }
```

with the property corresponding to the method included in the enumeration, which is most likely not what you want.

In general you want properties that correspond to data items or elements to be enumerable, but those that are methods and internal properties like size to be non-enumerable. By default every property is enumerable but you can control the inner workings of any property using the `defineProperty` or `defineProperties` methods of `Object` which were introduced in ES5.

For example, to set the format property to non-enumerable you simply add:

```
Object.defineProperty(myPerson,"format",{enumerable:false});
```

The `defineProperty` method will change any of the internal attributes of a property that you supply. Alternatively you can use the method to define the property and its internal attributes when creating the object in the first place. If you set format to non-enumerable then it will not appear in a `for in` loop. Notice that all properties supplied by the prototype mechanism are non-enumerable. This is another good reason for always defining methods on the prototype and properties on the instance.

You might be wondering why we didn't use `for of` in the previous example. If you try it you will quickly discover why. The `for in` loop iterates through the enumerable properties of the object, but the `for of` loop uses an iterator to access through the iterable properties of an object and custom objects don't have iterable properties unless you explicitly give them some. However some builtin objects do. For example, `Array`, `String`, `Map` and `Set` have iterable elements. This is a second solution to the same problem, but it is a more functionally-oriented solution.

Iterator - A Functional Approach To Loops

As we have seen, the key idea in enumeration is getting the next element in a collection of elements. In most cases it doesn't matter how that element is obtained, all we really need is a next function that returns the next element to be processed. This view of enumeration is a functionally-oriented one.

The idea is that an object that is iterable has a special method called `Symbol.iterator`. When called this returns an `iterator` object which has a next method. Each time the `next` method is called it returns an object with two properties - `value` and `done`. The `value` is the next element in the enumeration and `done` is `false` if there are more values and `true` if the enumeration is complete.

This may seem like an over complicated way of implementing a next function but it is more flexible than just demanding that an iterable has a next method. For example it makes a `for of` loop work with an iterable. What happens when you write a `for of` loop is that it first calls `Symbol.iterator` to get an iterator. It then calls the next method on that iterator, processing the value returned until `done` is `true`. The `for of` loop uses the same iterator for the entire loop. If you nest `for` `of` loops then each loop uses `Symbol.iterator` to get its own iterator. If you simply had a single next method you couldn't start another enumeration while one was in progress. Think of `Symbol.iterator` as an iterator factory.

To see this in action we can add a very trivial iterator to the name and phone number data structure:

```
const myPerson = {name: "mickey", phone: "123456" };
myPerson[Symbol.iterator] =
        function () {
            let position = 0;
            let that = this;
            return {next: function () {
                        position++;
                        if (position === 1)
                          return {done:false, value:that.name};
                        if (position === 2)
                          return {done:false, value:that.phone};
                        return {done: true, value: undefined}
                    }
                };
        };
```

This looks a little complicated because of the nested structure. The iterator is a function that returns an object that has a `next` method which is, of course, a function. The `next` method simply returns an object with `done` and `value` properties. It steps through the properties in a very simple way that is unlikely to be useful in a real program, but demonstrates that how you get each value in the enumeration is up to you. Notice that we have to store `this` for use when the `next` function is called. Also notice that `position` and `that` are accessible within the `next` function because of closure.

With this modification we can now write:

```
for (value of myPerson) {
   console.log(value);
}
```

and you will see the two values.

As well as `for` `of`, an iterable is required for the spread and destructuring operators and for other standard commands and expressions such as `Yield*` see the next section.

You can also call the iterator directly. For example:

```
const next=myPerson[Symbol.iterator]().next;
console.log(next());
console.log(next());
console.log(next());
```

displays:

```
{done: false, value: "mickey"}
{done: false, value: "123456"}
{done: true, value: undefined}
```

Generators and Iterables

Generators were introduced in ES2015 and they provide an easy way to create an iterable. A generator function can be written that returns a generator object, i.e. it is a generator object factory. A generator function is indicated by an asterisk after the function specifier:

```
function* genFactory(){
    yield 1;
    yield 2;
    yield 3;
}
```

and the yield command pauses and resumes the generator. The value specified as part of the yield is the value returned by the generator. When you call a generator it returns an iterator object complete with a next method. When you call the next method the generator function runs until it encounters the first yield when it returns the value as the result of the next method. When you call next again the generator resumes at the instruction following the yield and runs to the next yield and so on. For example:

```
const myGen=genFactory();

console.log(myGen.next());
console.log(myGen.next());
console.log(myGen.next());
console.log(myGen.next());
```

displays:

```
{value: 1, done: false}
{value: 2, done: false}
{value: 3, done: false}
{value: undefined, done: true}
```

You can see that a generator is an easy way to implement an iterator and:

```
for(value of myGen){
    console.log(value);
}
```

or:

```
for(value of genFactory()){
    console.log(value);
}
```

both display 1,2,3, as you would expect.

The key idea is that a generator creates an iterator and this means it can be used to add an iterator to any object in a much simpler way. For example, a generator-based iterator for our name and phone number object is easy:

```
myPerson[Symbol.iterator] = function () {
                           let that=this;
                           return function*(){
                                   yield that.name;
                                   yield that.phone;
                           }();
                    };
```

Now the generator specifies the iterator that is returned and we can just use yield to pause after each value has been returned. Notice that the generator is an immediately invoked function and it is the iterator that is returned, not the iterator factory.

If you use:

```
for (value of myPerson) {
    console.log(value);
}
```

you will once again see the two values.

There are many additional ways to use generators, but they all rely on the idea that a generator is an iterator factory.

Nearly Everything Is An Array

Objects are enumerable but, by default, not iterable. All built-in objects are both enumerable and iterable, There is a third possibility in that an object can be "array-like". To qualify as array-like an object has to have a length method and enumerable, index-based, properties.

For example:

```
let myArrayLike={length:3,2:"a",3:"b",4:"c"};

for(key in myArrayLike){
   console.log(key);
};
```

displays 2,3,4.

If you try for of you will discover that `myArrayLike` isn't iterable. We can make it iterable by adding an iterator, but it is much easier to use `Array.from` to convert it into a true array:

```
let myArrayLike={length:5,2:"a",3:"b",4:"c"};
myArrayLike=Array.from(myArrayLike);
for(value of myArrayLike){
   console.log(value);
};
```

which displays:

```
undefined
undefined
a
b
c
```

Notice that now we have to have `length` set to the number of elements in the `Array` including the undefined entries - `Array` objects don't have holes. The new `Array` object has all of the properties and methods of an `Array` and not just the iterator. You can also specify a function to be applied to each element after the `Array` like object has been converted to an `Array`.

Built-in objects can also be converted to arrays and in this case each element of the `Array` object is whatever the element is for the built-in object - i.e. for a `Map` it is an `Array` of [*key,value*] arrays.

Functional Strings

The `String` is an enumerable and iterable object, but it isn't an array of characters as it is in so many other languages. There is no explicit `String.map` and no `String.reduce`, for example and, while it is possible to scan through a `String` character by character, we tend not to. Strings are more usually manipulated by pulling them apart, inserting new strings and putting them back together. Of course, all of these operations can be achieved using loops, but the functional abstraction tends to be different from other iterables. There is also the matter that there is no fixed enumerable element for a `String`. Yes, some of the time you want to enumerate its characters, but often you want to enumerate words or sentences or some other meaningful unit like syllables or phonemes.

In short, `String` is an iterable you tend not to iterate, but you can if you want to.

For example, the `replace` method is usually thought of as a function that takes a substring or regular expression and searches for a match and then replaces that substring by one you have provided. For example:

```
const myString2=myString1.replace("target","replacement");
```

replaces `target` by `replacement` in the new `myString2`. Remember `String` objects are immutable so all string functions that seem to modify a string actually create a new string.

The `replace` method is in fact the `String` version of `map`, `filter` and `reduce`. The reason is that the first parameter can be a regular expression and the second can be a function. For example:

```
const myString="Hello World";
const myString2=myString.replace(/./g, function(match){
                                    return match.toUpperCase();
                                  }
                        );
console.log(myString2);
```

This scans the entire string character by character as the regular expression matches each and every character apart from line endings. If you want to include line endings use [^]. Each character in the string is passed to the function, as a `String`, and processed. Here it it converted to upper case. You can see that by changing the regular expression you can select which characters are processed by the function and hence implement `filter` or `reduce`.

Another way of doing the same thing is to use the `Array.from` method to convert the string into an array of single-character strings:

```
const myString = "Hello World";
const myArray=Array.from(myString);
console.log(myArray.map(function(element){
                          return element.toUpperCase();
                        }
                  )
          );
```

This produces:

```
["H", "E", "L", "L", "O", " ", "W", "O", "R", "L", "D"]
```

If you want the result to be put back together into a `String` use the `join` method:

```
console.log(myArray.map(function (element) {
                    return element.toUpperCase();
                }
                ).join("")
        );
```

Finally, if you want to enumerate and process a `String` as words you can use the `split` method:

```
const myString = "Hello World";
const myArray = myString.split(" ");
console.log(myArray.map(function (element) {
                    return element.toUpperCase();
                }
                ).join(" ")
        );
```

You can see that the functional approach to processing strings and arrays is very natural.

Function-Oriented Programming

When programmers first meet the functional approach to expressing iteration combined with fluent interfaces it generally creates an enthusiasm to explore functional programming. However, once the full list of functional programming rules and regulations are discovered the enthusiasm is often toned down. Many of the demands of functional programming are too difficult in a general purpose language and transitioning to a purpose-built functional language is difficult, if not impossible.

Then there is the issue that there is no proof that functional programming is desirable. The programmers who use it are convinced it is and will hear few criticisms that their approach might be flawed, let alone completely wrong. Functional programming attempts to ban mutable state and reduce programming to static mathematics, but dynamic change with time and the maintenance and mutation of state is what distinguishes programming from pure math and it could well be a big mistake to remove the essential character of programming in an effort to make it something it isn't.

What is clear is that, even with the help of a carefully crafted library, JavaScript isn't the best language for strict functional programming. It has excellent first class functions, but these are also objects which make them less than pure. You have the ability to make objects immutable, but it isn't easy to ensure that objects are immutable all the way down to their final values.

196

JavaScript supports recursion, but it has no automatic optimizations such as tail recursion allows. In addition, JavaScript is an asynchronous language and hence banishing mutable state when using callbacks, `Promises` or `async/await` is next to impossible.

In short, JavaScript has some functional features, but it isn't a functional language.

However, it isn't necessary to give up on the functional approach just because you can't go all the way. Using functions to wrap iteration and building pipelines of processes using fluent interfaces can result in programs that are easy to understand and this is good.

Sometimes this approach is called declarative programming because it seems to express what is to be done and not so much how to do it. You can see how:

```
myArray.map(myFunction);
```

is declarative in that it doesn't specify how `myFunction` is to be iterated across the array. However, this is declarative in a very small way. Most programmers have a model of how `map` and other iterative functions do their job in terms of working with each element in turn. True declarative programming leaves a lot more than just how an iteration is to be performed unspecified.

Making the maximum use of functions to create a compact expression of what you are doing is made easy in JavaScript. In this respect JavaScript is functionally-oriented. This indeed is a jem, but you need to be aware of the potential inefficiencies. When you use multiple calls to iterative functions you might be scanning the data structure multiple times when one pass would do the job if the loops were written out explicitly.

Jem 19

Metaprogramming - The Proxy

"A nice state of affairs when a man has to indulge his vices by proxy."

Raymond Chandler

Metaprogramming is strictly defined as being where code can be treated as data. JavaScript is a natural at metaprogramming because it can treat all code as data, even if this is generally frowned upon because it has many potential dangers - see Jem 10: Code as Data. As well as code being treated as data, metaprogramming also tends to mean doing things that change the way the language works and the new proxy object introduced in ES2015 arguably does this.

Whatever you want to call it, the `Proxy` object brings some much-needed capabilities to JavaScript, making it a jem in it's own right.

The Proxy Object

So what is a proxy? Put simply, a proxy is something that stands in for something else. In this case you can define a proxy for any JavaScript object and you can select what types of thing it will stand in for.

You create a `Proxy` object in the usual way:

```
const myProxy=new Proxy(target,handler);
```

where `target` is the object that the new object will proxy for. The second parameter is an object that defines the actions that the proxy will deal with and functions that define what happens. Any actions that are not defined in the `handler` are passed on to the `target`.

You can think of the `Proxy` as wrapping the `target` object and receiving a range of requests that would normally be handled automatically and allowing you to customize them. For example, you can use the get handler function to intercept any property retrieval. That is, the get function is called whenever a property of the target object is read and it can return a value for the property irrespective of what is actually stored in the target's property or even if the target has the property at all:

```
let myObject={myProperty:0};
const handler={get:function(target,prop,receiver){
                    return 42;
                }
        };
myObject = new Proxy(myObject, handler);
```

The parameters of the get function provide it with the target object, the property name and the receiver of the request - usually the `Proxy` object itself. You can see in this example that the get function returns 42, no matter what the property name is.

So if you try:

```
console.log(myObject.myProperty);
console.log(myObject.noProperty);
```

you will see 42 displayed for both properties, even though the first is set to 0 and the second doesn't actually exist.

In this case we wrapped the original object in a `Proxy` and lost the reference to it. This means we can only access the object via the proxy. However, if we had kept a reference to the original object:

```
myObject2 = new Proxy(myObject, handler);
```

then using `myObject2` would go via the proxy and `myObject` would use the properties of the original object without the interference of the proxy. That is, references to the proxy are intercepted, but references to the original object aren't. You can also revoke a `Proxy` object and after a `revoke` you can only access the original object.

Notice that this really is metaprogramming because you are modifying the default way that a property is accessed.

An alternative way of creating an object wrapped by a `Proxy` is to wrap a null object and then add properties:

```
const myObject=new Proxy({},handler);
myObject.myProperty=0;
```

This is a good approach to use in a constructor or an object factory.

Proxy objects also work within the prototype chain, for example:

```
const handler={get:function(target,prop, receiver){
                    return 42;
              }
          };
let myProxy=new Proxy({},handler);
const myObject=Object.create(myProxy,{myProperty:{value:0}});
console.log(myObject.myProperty);
console.log(myObject.noProperty);
```

In this case we create a proxy wrapping a null object and then create myObject with the proxy as its prototype. Now any properties defined on myObject are own properties and work as normal, i.e. myProxy does not intercept any uses of them, but any properties that are not own properties are searched for on the prototype chain and myProxy is invoked. As a result you see 0 displayed for myProperty and 42 for noProperty. In this case the receiver parameter is set to reference myObject rather than the wrapped null object.

You can also wrap built-in objects with a Proxy and this is very powerful.

Proxy Traps

Two of the easiest to understand proxy handlers, or traps as the documentation calls them, are get and set. We used get as the first example of using a Proxy in the previous section and set works in the same way, but intercepts any attempt to store something in a property:

```
get:function(target,prop, receiver)
set:function(target,prop, value, receiver)
```

Notice that both functions have the name of the property, prop and set also has the value being stored. The set function also has to return true if the value is written successfully and false otherwise. Also notice that unlike simple get and set accessor functions, proxy get and set intercept accesses to all properties. What this means is that you can use get and set to do things that are different for each property - tasks like validating, sanitizing and formatting data. You only need use the Proxy get and set if you need to modify the way a set or all the properties of an object are to behave i.e. a central approach to processing all properties.

So what sorts of things need Proxy get and set?

The most obvious application is to control what happens when you try to use a property that doesn't exist. By default if you try to retrieve a property that doesn't exist you get undefined. If you try to store a value in a property that doesn't exist then the property is created and the value stored. A more symmetric behavior would be to create the property when it is read with a default value. For example:

```
let myObject = {myProperty: 0};
const handler = {get: function (target, prop, receiver) {
                    if (target[prop] === undefined) {
                        target[prop]=null;
                    }
                    return target[prop];
                }
            };
```

In this case any property that doesn't exist, i.e. is undefined, is created and set to null. This means that if you try to get a value from a nonexistent property you get null and the property is created. If you try:

```
myObject=new Proxy(myObject,handler);
console.log(myObject.hasOwnProperty("noProperty"));
console.log(myObject.noProperty);
console.log(myObject.hasOwnProperty("noProperty"));
```

you will see false, null, and true indicating that the property doesn't exist, has a default value of null and exists, respectively. Notice that within the handler the Proxy is bypassed and that only accesses from JavaScript code, not internal accesses, use the Proxy. That is, hasOwnProperty bypasses the Proxy.

Using proxy get and set you can create a replacement for the deprecated non-standard watch method. You can even go much further, for example:

```
let myObject = {myProperty: 0};
const handler = {get: function (target, prop, receiver) {
                    console.log(prop+" read "+target[prop]);
                    return target[prop];
                },
            set: function(target,prop,value,receiver){
                    target[prop]=value;
                    console.log(prop+" write "+value);
                    return true;
                }
            };
myObject=new Proxy(myObject,handler);
```

This will display messages whenever a property is accessed. For example:

```
let a=myObject.myProperty;
myObject.myProperty=42;
```

results in:

```
myProperty read 0
myProperty write 42
```

You can also wrap built-in objects with a `Proxy`. For example, you can add negative index access to an array where myArray[-1] is the last element:

```
let myArray = [1, 2, 3, 4, 5, 6];
const handler = {get: function (target, prop, receiver) {
                    let index = +prop;
                    if (+prop < 0) {
                        index = target.length + (+prop);
                    }
                    return target[index];
                },
                set: function (target, prop, value, receiver) {
                    let index = +prop;
                    if (+prop < 0) {
                        index = target.length + (+prop);
                    }
                    target[index] = value;
                    return true;
                }
};
```

Notice that the `prop` parameter is always a string and so in this case you have to convert it to a number using (+prop).

An advanced application of Proxy set and get is in creating objects which get their properties from remote server calls. For example, you could set up an object with properties that were fetched from a web server only when they were requested. In this case you would probably want to return a `Promise` rather than the property.

The Proxy get and set methods are more powerful than the usual accessor get and set methods but you should use the accessor functions where possible. If you simply want to intercept the access to a small number of properties use the accessor methods. If you need to intercept the access before the accessor methods would be called, or want to intercept all accesses, then use the Proxy get and set.

Other Handlers

As well as set and get the Proxy object can intercept a range of other object access modes:

Trap	
getPrototypeOf()	A trap for Object.getPrototypeOf.
SetPrototypeOf()	A trap for Object.setPrototypeOf.
IsExtensible()	A trap for Object.isExtensible.
PreventExtensions()	A trap for Object.preventExtensions.
GetOwnPropertyDescriptor()	A trap for Object.getOwnPropertyDescriptor.
DefineProperty()	A trap for Object.defineProperty.
Has()	A trap for the in operator.
Get()	A trap for getting property values.
Set()	A trap for setting property values.
DeleteProperty()	A trap for the delete operator.
OwnKeys()	A trap for Object.getOwnPropertyNames and Object.getOwnPropertySymbols.
Apply()	A trap for a function call.
construct()	A trap for the new operator.

There are also constraints, called "invariants" in the documentation, that restrict what handlers can return, but these are mostly obvious. There is also a new Reflect object that has the same methods as Proxy, but implements the action on the specified object. For example:

```
let a=Reflect.get(target,prop);
```

returns the value of the property on the target. The Reflect object is mostly a tidying up of syntax involving Object.

While it is easy to understand what each of these do some of them present a problem in thinking up convincing use cases. Obviously, if you do want to customize the way that these internal JavaScript features behave, then this is the way to do it. Why you would want to change their behavior is more problematic. Some, however, do have immediate uses like get and set. Of the rest, the most interesting are apply and construct.

Proxy Apply

The apply method of the Proxy object allows you to intercept and service a function call on an object. It is called with the following parameters:

```
apply:function(target,this,argumentList)
```

The apply handler only works when the Proxy is wrapping a Function object, i.e. the target has to be callable. For example:

```
const handler = {apply: function(target,receiver,args){
                      console.log(target, receiver,args);
                      return target(...args);
                  }
              };
```

This handler will simply display the values of target, receiver and args and then call the function to pass the apply on to the wrapped Function object:

```
const myFunction=new Proxy(function(){
                      console.log("function called");
                  },handler);
myFunction("arg1","arg2");
```

displays:

```
ƒ (){console.log("function called");}
undefined
["arg1", "arg2"]
function called
```

It seems reasonable that you should only be able to use a proxy for apply with a Function object, but what about methods? How do you intercept a call to a method? This is trickier than you might think.

If you wrap an object with methods with an apply handler it doesn't intercept method calls. The reason is fairly obvious the apply handler only intercepts calls to the Function that it wraps not calls on properties that it might have. When you call a method first a property access occurs, potentially triggering a get handler and then an apply occurs but this doesn't trigger the apply handler in the same proxy.

For example:

```
const handler = {get: function (target, prop, receiver) {
                    console.log(prop + " read " + target[prop]);
                    return target[prop];
                }
        };
let myObject = {myProperty: 0};
myObject.test = function () {
                console.log("function called");
            };

myObject = new Proxy(myObject, handler);
myObject.test();
```

In this case the call to the test method is intercepted by the get handler and what you see is:

```
test read function () {
            console.log("function called");
        }
function called
```

Notice that returning the property:

```
return target[prop];
```

in the handler allows the method to be called, that is:

```
target[prop]();
```

If you want to modify a method call than you have to do it before returning the Function object's property. For example:

```
const handler = {get: function (target, prop, receiver) {
                    if (typeof target[prop] !== "function")
                                return target[prop];
                    return function (...args) {
                            console.log(prop + " function " +
                            target[prop]+" " + args);
                            return target[prop](...args);
                        };
                }
        };
```

The property being accessed is tested to see if it is a function. If it isn't then the property is returned. If it is a function then a new function is constructed, including parameters, and returned. This new function is then called by the apply that naturally follows the get when a method is called. Notice that the new function calls the original function as its return value.

This is a good way to intercept and modify method calls, but an alternative is to wrap the method's `Function` object with a `Proxy` directly:

```
const handler = {apply: function (target, receiver, args) {
                    console.log(target, receiver, args);
                    return target(...args);
                }
            };

let myObject = {myProperty: 0};
myObject.test = function () { console.log("function called"); };

myObject.test = new Proxy(myObject.test, handler);
myObject.test("arg1", "arg2");
```

We create a handler for `apply` and then use this to wrap the `test` method's `Function` object in a `Proxy`. What you see when this is run is:

```
ƒ () {
    console.log("function called");
  }
{myProperty: 0, test: Proxy}
["arg1", "arg2"]
function called
```

The advantage of wrapping the method with a `Proxy` is that you can intercept other actions using the appropriate handlers.

Proxy Construct

As we already know a constructor is a special sort of function object that is the subject of the `new` operator. The `construct` handler:

```
construct: function(target, args, newTarget)
```

is called whenever the `new` operator is used. For example:

```
const handler = {construct: function (target, args, newTarget) {
                    console.log(target);
                    console.log(args);
                    console.log(newTarget);
                    return {};
                }
            };
let myConstructor = function (){console.log("constructor called");};

myConstructor = new Proxy(myConstructor, handler);
const myObject = new myConstructor("arg1", "arg2");
```

This wraps a `myConstructor` with the `Proxy` and the `construct` handler.

What When you run the program you see:

```
ƒ () {
                console.log("constructor called");
            }
["arg1", "arg2"]
Proxy {length: 0, name: "myConstructor", arguments: null, caller:
null, prototype: {…}}
```

You can call the original constructor using:

```
target(...args);
```

or:

```
Reflect.construct(target,args)
```

For all of this to work, the target has to be a constructor, i.e. a Function that returns an object, and the newTarget, i.e. the proxy-wrapped constructor also has to be a constructor, i.e. a Function that returns an object.

Wrapping Problems

The idea of wrapping an existing object in a proxy is a very general one. Notice that once you have wrapped an existing object in a null Proxy you can still add add general properties and methods to it so as not to modify the object you have wrapped. For example:

```
let myObject = {};
let myObject2 = new Proxy(myObject, {
                set: function (target, prop, value, receiver) {
                    if (target[prop] === undefined)
                            this[prop] = value;
                    return true;
                },
                get: function (target, prop, receiver) {
                    if (target[prop] === undefined)
                            target=this;
                    return target[prop];
                }
            });
```

This works because within the handlers this is set to reference the Proxy and target references the wrapped object. The handlers simply check to see if the property is undefined on the target. If it is the property is created on the Proxy and its value returned on subsequent accesses.

If you try:

```
myObject2.myProperty = 42;
console.log(myObject.myProperty);
console.log(myObject2.myProperty);
```

you will discover that myObject doesn't have myProperty, but myObject2 does. You can use this approach to modify existing objects without changing the original and without making a copy.

Most of the problems that occur with using Proxy come down to problems with this. If the object being wrapped makes use of this in ways that aren't intercepted by the Proxy, then things won't work as you expect. The this value passed to the wrapped object references the Proxy and, for property accesses, this is reflected back to the original object, but if this is used in any other way, i.e. as a key or value in another object, then it won't work.

Index

214

JavaScript Bitmap Graphics with Canvas
ISBN: 978-1871962628

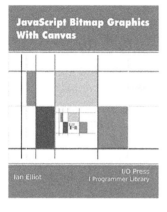

Since the introduction of Canvas into HTML, JavaScript has been a first class language for graphics allowing you to create graphics without resorting to a library of any kind.

This book by Ian Elliot is all about programming Canvas. Like many books and online resources, it covers the basics of using Canvas, but it also goes into many of the skills that you need to make good use of these facilities. For example, a graphics application often needs to download or upload files, but exactly how to do this in a modern way is difficult to find out. If you do upload a file then you might want to work with it at the pixel level and this requires working with raw binary data. How do you do this in JavaScript, which tries hard to keep data types hidden from the programmer?

Although most of the book is concerned with the standard 2D graphics context, the final chapters explain the use of WebGL with Canvas as a general purpose rendering engine, including how to use it for 3D graphics and for fast 2D graphics.

JavaScript Async: Events, Callbacks, Promises and Async Await
ISBN: 9781871962567

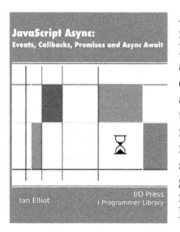

Asynchronous programming is essential to the modern web and at last JavaScript programmers have the tools to do the job – the Promise object and the async and await commands. These are so elegant in their design that you need to know about them if only to be impressed. It is likely that other languages will incorporate similar facilities in the future. While async and await make asynchronous code as easy to use as synchronous code there are a lot of subtle things going on and to really master the situation you need to know about Promises and you need to know how the JavaScript dispatch queue works.

Working with async can be confusing and disorienting, but by combining code examples and lucid explanations Ian Elliot presents a coherent explanation. If you want to work with async read this book first.

Just JavaScript: An Idiomatic Approach
ISBN: 9781871962574

Understand JavaScript for what it really is, a very different language that should not be compared to Java or dismissed as simply a scripting language. The book looks at the ideas that originally motivated the JavaScript approach and also at the additions over time that have produced modern language we now use.

This isn't a complete introduction to JavaScript and isn't for the complete beginner to programming. It has been written for those who are familiar with the basic constructs used in any programming language and have already encountered JavaScript. After reading Ian Elliot's account, you will have an understanding how and why JavaScript is unique and the ways in which you can exploit its strengths.

Just jQuery: The Core UI
ISBN:9781871962505

jQuery is a library of functions for JavaScript that provides easy and sophisticated access to the HTML in a web page. Originally intended to smooth over the differences in the way browsers interact with JavaScript, it has developed into a much more powerful tool that fully lives up to its motto of "write less, do more". As a result jQuery is compact and can seem cryptic until you get used its common idioms.

Written for JavaScript developers working with web page layout, this book enables you to use jQuery easily and efficiently. It also cuts through its seeming complexity, by presenting enough explanation at every stage for you to understand what is happening.

Just jQuery: Events, Async & Ajax
ISBN: 9781871962529

Written for JavaScript developers working with advanced web pages this book covers the parts of jQuery not associated with the DOM. Specifically it is about how to make use of jQuery's event functions, Deferred and Promise functions and its AJAX functions. While not every programmer will need these advanced features in the early stages of using JavaScript, they are unavoidable aspects of modern web programming and sooner or later you will find a need to master them all.

This book is about ideas. Ian Elliot shows you how to use jQuery, but mainly by explaining how jQuery approaches the task. Once you understand this there is little need to go over complicated examples where the problem is seeing the big ideas because the small detail is overwhelming.

www.ingramcontent.com/pod-product-compliance
Lightning Source LLC
LaVergne TN
LVHW062315060326
832902LV00013B/2223